Surviving the Second Great Depression

How to Take Advantage of the Government That Is Trying to Take Advantage of You

by J.S.B. Morse

Surviving the Second Great Depression: How to Take Advantage of the Government That Is Trying to Take Advantage of You. Copyright © 2009 by Joseph Morse. All Rights Reserved. Printed in the United States of America. No part of this book may be used or reproduced in any manner whatsoever without written consent by the author. Exceptions are granted for brief quotations within critical articles or reviews.

This book was produced by Amelior Publishing Company, an imprint of Code Publishing, San Diego, CA. www.code-interactive.com/amelior

ISBN 1-60020-045-1

978-1-60020-045-8

Contents

Part One: Introduction   1
   Prozac Nation   6
   Define Your Terms   10
   The Sky Is Falling…and Falling   17

Part Two: The Techniques   25
   Fight the Fed's Whoopee Cushion   25
   Refinance Or Don't   32
   Downsize Your Life   38
   Invest In Your Future   42
   Grab a Grant   49
   Capitalize on Unemployment Insurance (That's Why We Have It!)   52
   Avoid It Like the Plague   58
   Itemize   61
   Start a Business   64
   Move to Greener Pastures   69
   Take It Off Shore   71
   Find a Lasting Solution   78

Part Three: Conclusion   85
Notes   91
Bibliography   93

Part One
Surviving the Second Great Depression

"The only thing we have to fear is fear itself."
- Franklin D. Roosevelt

"The only thing we have to fear
is a government trying to instill fear in us."
- Anonymous

There are a lot of problems with government, but one problem is very striking and not very well publicized. Government officials, by the nature of their job, are perpetually deciding what to do with other people's money. Since that is the case, it is understandable that those officials want to take their time drafting legislation—after all, we're disgruntled enough that they're taking our money at all; it would be much worse if we thought they were careless with that money. But the understandably lengthy process to conceive of a government initiative, frame it in the form of a legal doctrine, and then move it through the approval and implementation processes makes government extremely inefficient.

For example, during the recent downturn in the economy,

presidential candidates argued over whether they should halt the federal gasoline tax in order to alleviate the burden that high gas prices were causing on most Americans. John McCain and Hillary Clinton wanted to halt the tax and Barack Obama scoffed at the notion because it would only mean a $30 savings and gas companies would just charge more anyway. Well, I don't know if Barack Obama is qualified enough to claim that $30 in savings is too small for each citizen, but perhaps he had a better plan. In fact he did. Typical of his campaign stump speech at the time, Obama said in April, 2008 that, "[We] need a president who can stand up to Big Oil and big energy companies and say enough is enough." What that means is fairly ambiguous, but what that implies is that Obama was going to force oil companies to make gasoline cheaper.

Well, as the campaign drew on, the rhetoric increased but nothing along the lines of telling Big Oil that enough is enough ever occurred. The government didn't reduce its tax on oil and no one in government went to the offices of Big Oil and demanded lower prices.

Yet, the prices fell. Gas prices fell so dramatically, in fact, that a gallon of petrol was as cheap as it's been for a decade in early 2009. We were buying gas for $1.60 a gallon for a while in California—usually one of the most expensive places to buy gas! Gas prices fell so fast and so furious that the political chatter about the energy crisis, so loud a few months before, was completely gone by the 2008 election.

How did gas prices fall so precipitously if it wasn't for government intervention? Gas prices fell because the market controlled them and the market didn't want to pay $5 a gallon any more, it wanted to pay $2 a gallon. Some might say that sounds like magic—why would gas companies just drop their prices? They could charge whatever they wanted. There must be someone pulling the strings back there making the prices change, the skeptic might claim. Well, there isn't some*one* pulling the strings and making gas prices change, there are 6 billion people pulling the strings. When people began to feel the

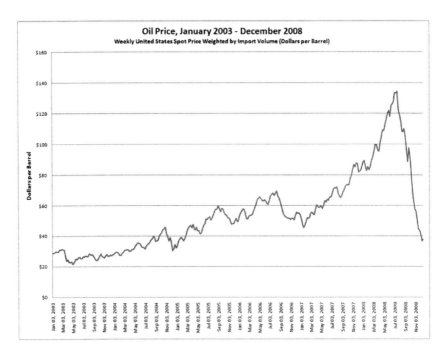

Figure 1. Oil prices fell as a reaction to the market without government intervention

financial crunch in 2007, they started cutting back on road trips, flights to exotic destinations, and cruises around the world. They walked to the grocery store instead of driving there. They thought twice before making a wasted trip to the office. Ultimately, everyone reduced their demand for gas and gas companies reacted. Once people stopped buying gas, the gas companies stopped buying oil and the price of crude fell. After crude plummeted, gas stations were able to be flexible with their pricing. One station on an island in the middle of a lonely suburb named Oak Dale somewhere in America lowered its prices a nickel, then, not to be undersold, the station across the street lowered its prices six cents. The stations down the street then lowered their prices, and eventually, the market found a reasonable price where supply equaled demand.

My point here isn't that the gas tax is wrong or that gas prices should be under $2; my point is that government didn't need to do anything to "fix" the energy crisis; it fixed itself. Government is too slow and cumbersome to do anything like what the market did on its own in 2008 and this applies not only to gas prices, but to everything government is involved with, including "fixing" the economic crisis. In fact, government intervention throughout history has not only failed to do what it was designed to do, but it usually ends up making the situation worse, as we'll see throughout this book.

Still, because few people are aware of government's inherent impotence in matters of the economy, we have politicians (on both sides of the aisle, of course) who think it's government's duty to intervene, regulate, and promote various things throughout society and the economy. With regard to the financial crisis of 2008, there have been many propositions to save the economy—all involving coercion by the government and all completely unnecessary to fix the economy.

Some would say that we need the government to step up because certain companies are "too big to fail" or the government is the only behemoth with the spending power to turn the economy around. Well, I say that if a company was too big to fail, it was probably artificially inflated (most likely by government backing or subsidies) in the first place, and if government is the only thing that can save us in this economy, we're going to need something even bigger to save us from government.

So, we find ourselves in a predicament in which most Americans irrationally think that government policies, as slow and inefficient as they are, can identify and solve the problems our country faces, more quickly and efficiently than the free market can. Most Americans are afraid of economic collapse. We enjoy our SUVs, our trips to Cancún, and our nights on the town and we don't want to lose them. We may not enjoy our jobs, but we certainly think we need them in order to get us those luxuries, and so we're afraid of losing those pesky occupations. And if the government can ensure those things, most of us don't really care what it takes—$4 trillion dollar federal budgets, $2 trillion deficits, higher taxes across the board, whatever.

As a result of our fear, the government is taking advantage of us, and, to a large extent, our future selves and children. Officials in the government are telling us that we need to be afraid, but that they can solve everything with their smartly applied trillions. And since people see government as the only way to "solve" the economic problems we face, those in government naturally react like a monopoly and push the price of their "solutions" through the roof. It's the same with any monopoly. Just imagine if there was only one place we could get water or mp3 players or gasoline; prices for those items would be ridiculously high—about as high as government products, perhaps.

Government officials benefit from this system because as long as they are seen as the savior, their jobs, and salaries are safe while the rest of America gets laid off. And as long as government officials are in control, the special interests that got them there are going to be rewarded first. Some other Americans may also benefit, but they probably aren't the deserving ones and they're more like an excuse for government involvement, not the reason for it. For example, many deserving people probably receive welfare from the federal government, but many of the recipients are naturally just abusing the system to avoid responsibility. And the more that people are dependent on the financial aid of the government, the more the government sees that as a reason to extend more benefits, exacerbating the situation.

In essence, we're stuck with an overbearing government that is taking advantage of our fear of economic collapse and making us pay for solutions that aren't really solutions. Through forced bailouts and stimulus packages, we're supporting broken companies and financial systems and thereby making the situation worse. So much worse, that it appears that we're heading into another Great Depression. Sure there might be a little hyperbole involved in the title, but the comparison is apt. The fall of the stock market in 2008 was the largest (by percent) than any other year that kicked off a recession. The fall in housing prices in 2008 was unprecedented. And the rise in unemployment was equally shocking. With all of these factors considered, it may well be that we're in the midst of the Second Great Depression.

I realize I'm starting to sound like a real Debbie Downer here, but we need to recognize what's going on before we can realize what we can do to correct the situation. Eventually, most Americans will realize that more government control doesn't mean more economic success (or even more happiness for that matter). It may take a complete collapse of the governmental system as it did with the Soviet Union (one of the most controlling governments of all time), but eventually it will happen. In the mean time, we, as rational citizens continue to spread the word that bigger government is not the solution, and in fact, is the problem. We can also start to take advantage of the people who are taking advantage of us. In this case, the people taking advantage of us are the government officials who have been putting our livelihoods on the line to support broken companies based on our fears that we'll lose our livelihoods if we don't. This book is about those people and the ways that we can take advantage of the government that is trying to take advantage of us.

Prozac Nation

In 1873, Jay Cooke and Company, a leading bank at the time, failed and sent the United States into an economic depression that lasted years. When the major bank couldn't pay for some obligations they had made with Northern Pacific Railway, rumors began to circulate that Cooke's credit had become worthless. The bank went bankrupt shortly after and set off a series of bankruptcies in the country.

Starting on September 20th of that year, the New York Stock Exchange was halted and didn't resume until after ten days. Then things got bad. Nearly a quarter of the nation's railroads went bankrupt;

a total of 18,000 businesses failed. Unemployment skyrocketed to fourteen percent as construction work lagged and wages were cut. Real estate values took a dive and corporate profits disappeared. It was what became known as the "Long-Wave Depression" and it certainly took a toll on the country.

But the government didn't pass any $800 billion stimulus packages like the current Congress seems to enjoy doing, nor did it create gigantic government projects like the Tennessee Valley Authority or Social Security like Roosevelt's government did. The federal government did relatively nothing during the Long-Wave Depression compared to the governments of the 1930s and today. In fact, federal expenditures *decreased* during the depression. Yet the economy recovered.

A similar financial panic occurred two decades later in 1893 when a railroad bubble similar to the dot com bubble of the 1990s came

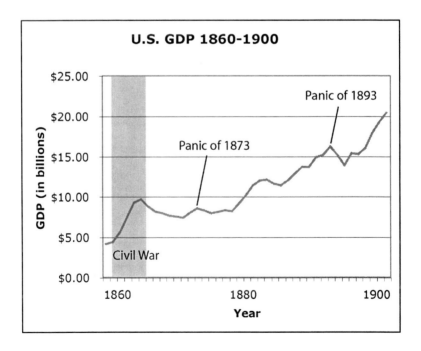

Figure 2. After the Civil War, economic recessions were regular but minor dips in the growth of the American economy.

crashing down. The Philadelphia and Reading Railroad went bankrupt after greatly overextending itself and led to a domino effect of bankruptcies and business failures that were fueled by a run on banks. This time again, unemployment skyrocketed (to nearly 20%) and many companies associated with the railroad boom went out of business. Again, the federal government did relatively little to "fix" the economy (compared with the actions of the Roosevelt-, Bush-, and Obama-led governments), but the financial system turned around within two years and a ten-year economic boom took place once confidence was restored.

Until 1907, that is, when another financial panic occurred, sending the country into yet another economic depression. The 1907 version of economic crisis also contained a recovery that was absent of much government intrusion. After all, the federal government, led by Teddy Roosevelt was too busy sending its "Great White Fleet" around the world in a show of power to do anything about the financial panic.

Economies naturally rise and fall in a cycle involving peaks and troughs of various sectors throughout. Economic cycles include four stages: expansion, prosperity, contraction, and recession, which occur in order and repeat. The recessions and depression throughout the history of the United States generally followed this cycle naturally and the country grew from an insignificant neophyte to become the most economically powerful nation in the history of the world even despite recurrent recessions and (perhaps especially) without much government intervention.

Perhaps it was a good thing, too, that the government failed to intervene in these instances. After all, every time policymakers did intervene, things took a turn for the worse. When Congress passed the Coinage Act of 1873, for instance, the U.S. stopped using silver to back its currency, which led to a deflation of silver prices and artificially altered the weight of debt in the country. Western miners, who were effected most by the Coinage Act, called it "The Crime of '73." The move

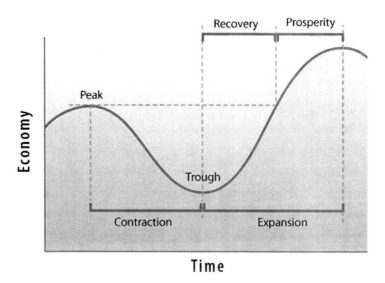

Figure 3. Economies naturally cycle through expansion and contraction. Artificial interference with this cycle may produce exaggerrated effects (higher peaks and longer troughs).

reduced the money supply and put stress on gold as the lone metal backing the American currency.

Nearly twenty years later government action again hurt the economy. The Sherman Silver Purchase Act of 1890 reversed the Coinage Act of 1873 and required the government to buy silver with Treasury notes. This plan backfired by causing the currency to inflate. Also, investors simply traded in their silver notes for gold notes and depleted the government's gold reserves.

No government intervention was as disruptive as what followed the depression of 1907, however. The stakes were high at the time; banker Jacob Schiff warned that, "This country is going to undergo the most severe and far reaching money panic in its history." The solution that many, including Schiff, produced was to create a United States central bank that would be able to lend money out in times of financial panic. So, the biggest names in New York banking got together and tried to organize such a central bank. One would think that Americans at large would encourage such a plan in order to save the country from economic disaster, but the big-name bankers weren't acting like that would be the case. The meeting on Jekyll Island, S.C. between wealthy tycoons wasn't a heavily publicized or especially transparent; as B.C. Forbes wrote some time later:

> Picture a party of the nation's greatest bankers stealing out of New York on a private railroad car under cover of darkness, stealthily riding hundreds of miles South, embarking on a mysterious launch, sneaking onto an island deserted by all but a few servants, living there a full week under such rigid secrecy that the names of not one of them was once mentioned, lest the servants learn the identity and disclose to the world this strangest, most secret expedition in the history of American finance. I am not romancing; I am giving to the world, for the first time,

Define Your Terms

This might be a good place to actually define the terms recession and depression so as to set the stage for what we're facing in our modern economy. An economic recession is a period of time in which a particular country's economy retracts for at least two quarters of the year. In other words, if the Gross Domestic Product of Albania goes from $10.62 billion in January to $10.5 billion in March and $10.4 billion in June, Albania is officially in a recession. The National Bureau of Economic Research (NBER) defines an economic recession as, "a significant decline in [the] economic activity spread across the country, lasting more than a few months, normally visible in real GDP growth, real personal income, employment (non-farm payrolls), industrial production, and wholesale-retail sales."

In early 2009, seven economists from the NBER announced that after 11 months of research, they've determined what everyone else in America already had felt with pink slips or stock losses: we were in fact in a recession. According to data from the Bureau of Economic Analysis (BEA), the U.S. economy shrunk by a seasonally-adjusted annual rate of 0.2% in the last quarter of 2007, then rose slightly the next two quarters the real story of how the famous Aldrich currency report, the foundation of our new currency system, was written.

The brainchild of the Jekyll Island bunch was the Federal Reserve (the Fed), a central bank that would be able to limit the United States to one currency (there were thousands of currencies in circulation before the Federal Reserve existed) and control that currency to maintain its value and prevent the runs on banks that caused the financial panics of 1873, 1893, and 1907. The Fed, which was approved by congress in 1913 (with over a quarter of Congress absent), was designed to maintain a healthy economy with three tools: an elastic currency, a check-clearing system, and a lender of last resort. Federal bureaucrats were busy that

---

only to fall again in the third and fourth quarters of 2008 ((-0.5%, and -6.2%, respectively—the 6.2% drop being the worst since 1982)). That means we're in a recession, officially, but is talk of a depression warranted, and, if so, is talk of another "Great Depression" necessary?

Well, NBER doesn't chime in on economic depressions (they only label economic recessions) and economists haven't really come to any explicit way to differentiate a depression from a recession, but most people agree that a depression is just a long recession. Some say that depressions are just recessions with abnormally high unemployment, restriction of credit, shrinking output and investment, numerous bankruptcies, reduced amounts of trade and commerce, as well as highly volatile relative currency value fluctuations, mostly devaluations. By that standard, then, we are in a depression and there's no light at the end of the tunnel since all of these indicators show no sign of reversing their downward trends.

From our brief history of U.S. recessions in the previous section and the synopsis of our current economic climate in the next, you will see that we're in a dire state, and the busy-ness that federal government officials are creating isn't helping the situation. It appears that we've collectively shot ourselves in the foot and we're using the same gun to get the first bullet out.

year as it was the same year that congressmen changed the Constitution and allowed the federal government to tax income (federal income tax had only been active during the Civil War previously).

To glimpse the effects of these developments, let us examine a few of the major components. First off, the dawn of the Federal Reserve meant that competing currencies within the United States had seen their last light. Before 1913, there were 30,000 different currencies floating around in America and there was no central control over any of them. The Fed said that there should only be one currency in this country and it should be an elastic currency. An elastic currency is one that can expand or contract in an amount warranted by economic conditions. In other words, the Fed was allowed to inject more money into the economy or take it out to inflate or deflate the currency and stabilize the financial system. A check-clearing system is one that mandated all banks clear checks from other financial institutions—even in times of crisis. The Federal Reserve also had the authority to act as a lender of last resort—the ability to lend to banks that no other banks would lend to presumably because the risk was too high.

Looking at the ideas in context of the previous financial panic, they seem reasonable and looked like they would do the trick to prevent recessions and depressions. Call it Prozac for a depressed national economy. But a funny thing about the pharmaceutical Prozac also applies to the government solutions. Studies have found that while Prozac does help a segment of the population from their symptoms of depression, a completely inert placebo helps the same percentage from their symptoms also. In other words, it's not the Prozac that helps; it's the feeling of doing something to help yourself that actually works. In the case of the government solutions, it's not Federal Reserve that got us out of the depression of 1907, it was the idea that things were being done to help the economy.

The result of the Federal Reserve was to take much of the freedom out of investing and banking to ensure stability. After all, Americans shouldn't have to put up with all of those bank scares every couple decades, proponents would argue. We needed to stop the treacherous contractions in the economy, so, by prescribing the Federal Reserve, the government took steps to do just that. And it worked.

That is, it worked right up until the next depression hit just sixteen years later. This time, the depression was much worse than the previous ones; it was dubbed the Great Depression and lasted twice as long as previous downturns. Some have said that poor banking decisions and the unregulated financial boom of the Roaring Twenties were what made the Great Depression as bad as it was—a reasonable notion considering the frenzied picture we get from that decade. But most economists disagree. The Great Depression was the end of a regular financial cycle—a contraction in the economy just like the previous depressions—but government intervention (the side effects of economic

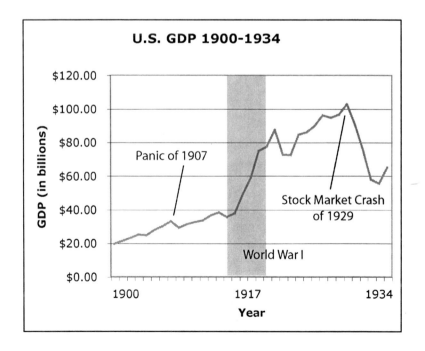

Figure 4. After the Fed started manipulating the economy, the growth and contraction of the American economy was magnified.

Prozac) exacerbated the damage done by the natural economic cycle and the regular cyclical trough turned into a canyon.

It could rightly be said that poor banking decisions and unsustainable stock-trading policies happened in each depression from 1873 to the "Great" one in the 1930s, but only after the Fed was meddling in the economy were those poor banking decisions exacerbated by the increased monetary weight of the American taxpayer. In other words, people thought they could make worse than usual mistakes because the taxpayer would cover them. Also, in order to stabilize the economy, the Fed had inflated the currency in the '20s unnaturally (mainly to help Britain's economy after World War I). This inflation had the effect of amplifying those poor banking and stock decisions. It turns out that the Federal Reserve System didn't prevent depressions from happening, it just magnified the consequences.

And once the depression had hit, further government intervention (much of it in the form of Roosevelt's New Deal) made matters worse. The Smoot-Hawley Tariff Act raised tariffs on 20,000 imported goods and prompted other countries to raise tariffs on American goods, ultimately killing foreign trade. In addition, Roosevelt signed Executive Order 6102, which made the private ownership of gold illegal and shook the idea of private ownership. As historian Robert Higgs said this government intervention created, "pervasive uncertainty among investors about the security of their property rights in the their capital and its prospective returns," the very foundation on which a modern economy is based.

One of the New Deal programs that boggles the mind in its ludicrousness is the Agricultural Adjustment Administration, designed, as its name implies, to alter the farm system. It's difficult to imagine why, but somebody in the Roosevelt administration thought it was a good idea to pay farmers NOT to produce food on their land. With this scheme, farmers were paid subsidies to leave their land barren, thus reducing crop outputs and increasing the prices of those crops. Not only did the monumentally wasteful program pay people for negative production, it also created a shortage of goods, which, by 1935 was alleviated by importing 35 million bushels of corn (up from 4 million bushels a decade earlier). No wonder why consumers were, "horrified with [this] policy of enforced scarcity."

But most of the country wasn't concerned about property rights, prospective stock returns, or even what farmers were or were not planting in the 1930s; many were worried about finding work so that they could feed their families. So, afraid of starvation, Americans welcomed in the pinnacle of the Progressive Era, the New Deal. Envisioned by Hoover and put into action by Franklin Roosevelt, the New Deal included a tidal wave of government programs designed to take some of the fiscal power away from business (increased income taxes and corporate taxes, institution of the Securities and Exchange Commission) and give it to the people (Social Security, Agriculture Adjustment Act).

Despite all the unintentionally harmful efforts by government, the U.S. Gross Domestic Product finally returned to its pre-Depression level in 1939—ten years after the stock market crash that triggered it. And those efforts weren't cheap. Government expenditures nearly doubled from 1930 to 1931 in order to pay for all the programs and almost quadrupled from pre-Depression to post-Depression years. As Roosevelt's Secretary of the Treasury said in 1939 about what he considered the failed New Deal, "We tried spending money. We are spending more than we have ever spent before and it does not work.... We have never made good on our promises....I say after eight years of this Administration we have just as much unemployment as when we started....and an enormous debt to boot!"

But Progressive apologists would disagree, those costs were worth it, they would say. We needed to inflate the size of government to stop the economic depression and to prevent future ones! But economic contractions didn't stop after the federal government

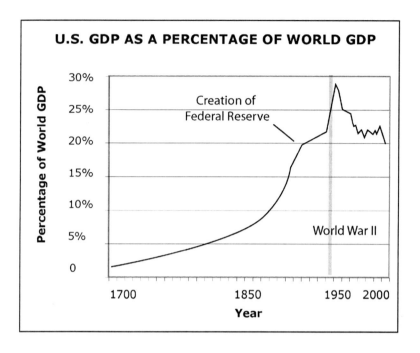

Figure 5. The United States economy grew exponentially until the creation of the Federal Reserve. Since the Fed's creation, the GPD of the United States as a percentage of the World GDP has leveled off.

quadrupled its size and regulation. After the Great Depression, a recession or depression started in the years 1937, '39, '48, '53, '57, '60, '69, '73, '80, '81, '90, '01, and of course 2008. What's more, contractions happened just as often and were just as severe than they were before the Fed began its interference (measured in production months, the average per recession before 1919 was 1.3, between 1920 and 1939 it was 7.8, and since then it has been 1.3 on average). According to the data, it seems that the massive government intervention of the New Deal didn't prevent economic contractions at all; it just ensured your taxes were going to be higher.

Along the way, the constant intervention in the American economy by its government has had other contrary effects. It cost the American public trillions upon trillions of dollars to support government intrusion into the market through taxation, artificial currency control, and subsidies, and it has not even done what its architects intended it to do, stabilize the economy. Today, we're again faced with a serious recession—perhaps even a depression—and it makes one wonder if we could have gotten this crisis without making our currency practically worthless through inflation (one of the Fed's brilliant policies) and taxing about a third of what's left. If certain federal government programs and the Fed in particular haven't been able to do what they were designed to do, isn't it time we start asking what the point of their existence is?

The Sky Is Falling...and Falling

When I was a kid and I played with someone else's toy and broke it, my mom would make me pay for it. Today, when government plays with someone else's toy and breaks it, they don't pay for it—they force everyone else to pay for it. What's more is that the toys that the federal government is playing with today aren't $5 G.I. Joe action figures, they are multi-trillion-dollar mortgage companies.

Over the past thirty or so years, your federal government has passed a series of laws, created a number of bureaucracies, and generally intruded into the financial markets at an astounding rate. So much so that anyone who claims that we have been participating in a free-market economy all this time is fooling himself. Below is a survey of the government programs—or toys, as some Washington bureaucrats might regard them as—that have arisen over the last few decades and which have contributed substantially (if not completely) to the current financial crisis we find ourselves wallowing in.

Some politicians, like the ever-illuminating Nancy Pelosi, and the "didn't know there was an economic crisis" John McCain claim that this recession is a result of big corporation greed. But that seems like a cop out to me. As policy analyst Lawrence White contested, if a high number of airplanes crashed one year, do we blame gravity? Greed, White said, is like gravity, it's always there. No, something else set off this nasty financial situation and it just so happens that the ones blaming greed as the cause certainly played their part in the mess. In general, it wasn't free-market business or even greed that caused our recession; it was reckless government intervention.

With regard to this recession, a slew of government intervention was kicked off in 1968 with the metamorphosis of Fannie Mae from a government-run secondary mortgage company to a private shareholder-run (though still government-backed) secondary mortgage company. The goal of Fannie Mae (and its later accomplice Freddie Mac) was to purchase mortgages from retail mortgage lenders in order to "provide stability" in the secondary mortgage market—a great-sounding goal if there ever was one.

About eight years later, Congress passed the Community Reinvestment Act (CRA), which was designed to combat discrimination by mortgage lenders. The goal of the act was to provide everyone with fair mortgage lending opportunities, regardless of race or sex—another worthy goal.

In 1992, the Federal Housing Enterprises Financial Safety and Soundness Act was passed and forced Fannie Mae and Freddie Mac to devote a percentage of their lending to support affordable housing (meaning they would promote loans with lower interest rates or interest-only plans that result in lower monthly payments, thus making them "affordable"). This act resulted in Fannie Mae purchasing $2 billion in "MyCommunityMortgage" loans by 2000. MyCommunityMortgage loans are defined on Fannie Mae's website as 40-year loans requiring only 3% down and interest-only options. The loans were also required to be flexible on credit history; in other words, these "sub-prime" loans were to be given to people who probably wouldn't have been able to get a loan otherwise (borrowers with a credit score of 680 or less). But no one in Fannie Mae or its bureaucratic sponsor, the federal government, cared to ask if it was wise to offer loans to people who shouldn't be getting loans. Instead, they just increased the practice. In 2001, Fannie Mae had announced that they had acquired $10 billion in specially targeted CRA loans and set a goal of acquiring $500 billion in those loans by 2010.

By this time it was clear that there was a concerted effort by the federal government to help unqualified borrowers get home loans that they normally wouldn't have gotten. The new CEO of Fannie Mae under the Clinton administration, Harold Raines said, "Fannie Mae has expanded home ownership for millions of families in the 1990s by reducing down payment requirements." And boy did they expand home ownership! Backed by the U.S. taxpayer, Fannie controlled 43 percent of the mortgage market by 2001. By the time the financial crisis hit, that share was equivalent to nearly $800 billion for Fannie and Freddie each.

The overall result was that mortgage companies sold loans to buyers they knew could not afford to pay back those loans. Why? Because government-backed Fannie Mae was eager to take the loans off the hands of the banks. The situation was compounded when the U.S. Department of Housing and Urban Development said it would dedicate 50% of its business to low- and moderate-income families (many of which fell into the sub-prime category described above). Backed by the American taxpayer, government officials increased the amount of sub-prime loans on the books to problematic levels. Russell Roberts painted the bleak picture in the *Wall Street Journal*:

> Beginning in 1992, Congress pushed Fannie Mae and Freddie Mac to increase their purchases of mortgages going to low- and moderate-income borrowers. For 1996, the Department of Housing and Urban Development (HUD) gave Fannie and Freddie an explicit target—42 percent of their mortgage financing had to go to borrowers with income below the median in their area. The target increased to 50 percent in 2000 and 52 percent in 2005.

For 1996, HUD required that 12 percent of all mortgage purchases by Fannie and Freddie be "special affordable" loans, typically to borrowers with income less than 60% of their area's median income. That number was increased to 20% in 2000 and 22% in 2005. The 2008 goal was to be 28%. Between 2000 and 2005, Fannie and Freddie met those goals every year, funding hundreds of billions of dollars worth of loans, many of them sub-prime and adjustable-rate loans, and make to borrowers who bought houses with less than 10% down.

In 2007, before the financial crisis hit, George W. Bush's Federal Reserve Chairman, Ben Bernanke proposed further increases of Freddie and Fannie into the affordable housing market. In other words, he wanted the government to back even more sub-prime loans and increase the size of the two mortgage behemoths.

This explosion of the government-backed financial institutions was only possible due to the monumentally misguided policy of our old friend from 1913, the Federal Reserve System. Policy analyst Lawrence H. White summed up the situation perfectly in his paper, *How Did We Get into This Financial Mess?*:

> In the recession of 2001, the Federal Reserve System, under Chairman Alan Greenspan, began aggressively expanding the U.S. money supply. Year-over-year growth in the M2 monetary aggregate rose briefly above 10 percent, and remained above 8 percent entering the second half of 2003. The expansion was accompanied by the Fed repeatedly lowering its target for the federal funds (interbank short-term) interest rate. The federal funds rate began 2001 at 6.25 percent and ended the year at 1.75 percent. It was reduced further in 2002 and 2003, in mid-2003 reaching a record low of 1 percent, where it stayed for a year. The real Fed funds rate was negative—meaning that nominal rates were lower than the contemporary rate of inflation—for two and a half years. In purchasing-power terms, during that period a borrower was not paying but rather gaining in proportion to what he borrowed.

And economist Steve Hanke added, "This set off the mother of all liquidity cycles and yet another massive demand bubble." Nice work Alan.

The intent of this government intrusion into the free market was good; the Clinton and Bush administrations (along with Greenspan and Bernanke) wanted more people to own a home and enjoy a larger slice of the American pie. However, it's clear that their policy was misguided. Allowing more people to purchase homes increased the demand, which—no surprise—made home prices skyrocket. The government's policies inflated the housing bubble that saw 20-plus percent gains in home values year after year from 2004 to 2007, making it more difficult for everyone to buy a home. In addition, government policies saddled banks and mortgage companies with trillions of dollars in risky debt that became "toxic" debt once the housing and credit markets began to tighten up when the bubble burst.

People across the country bought houses they knew they couldn't afford and, thanks to the government sponsored enterprises (GSEs) of Fannie Mae and Freddie Mac, they were able to take out loans that they couldn't pay back. The plan for many of these homeowners was to buy the house, squeeze by with the payments for as long as possible, then sell the house for a 20% gain within a year or so—a procedure called "flipping." And the plan was fine as long as housing prices continued to go up as fast as they were in the middle of the decade. But housing prices were only going up so much because the demand was so high, and demand was so high because there were so many new people in the market (thanks to the artificially lenient government policies). When this demand began to slow down, the housing prices rose slower and homeowners weren't able to make the money they had hoped to make on their investments. What comes up must come down, and boy did housing prices come down! Like a lead balloon, the prices came falling down in 2007 and continued plummeting through the time of this writing. Once prices began to fall, people found themselves with loans worth more than the value of their homes (they were up-side down) and a tsunami of foreclosures started to engulf the country.

An unprecedented amount of foreclosures (estimates place the number at 3 million) hit the entire financial sector affecting what is called thrift lenders—those who provided cheap mortgages like MyCommunityMortgages (Washington Mutual, Wachovia, Countrywide). The foreclosures hit Fannie Mae and Freddie Mac most dramatically, however. After all, those were the GSEs that had instigated this sub-prime buying craze, and they were left with much of the leftover "toxic" loans. Stockholders began to recognize the problem in late 2007 and drove the stock price of both the companies from over $60 to $.30 a share within a year. To put that into perspective, the two companies lost the wealth equivalent to the entire Gross Domestic Product the state of Nevada in less than twelve months.

The crunch that started in mortgage-related financial institutions like Fannie and Freddie soon spread to general financial companies like Citi and Bank of America, both of which saw a slashing of stock prices following announcements of multi-billion dollar writedowns (the acknowledged loss in value of an asset). And once the entire financial landscape was affected by the financial crisis, the banks went into defensive survival mode—ushering in the credit crisis we're all too familiar with today. Lending became rare and costly despite the Fed's incessant lowering of interest rates and very few people could get money to do anything.

But it's not like this collapse was a surprise. As the New York Times writer Steven A. Holmes predicted in an article in 1999 about the risky government intervention, "In moving, even tentatively, into this new area of lending, Fannie Mae is taking on significantly more risk, which may not pose any difficulties during flush economic times. But the government-subsidized corporation may run into trouble in an economic downturn, prompting a government rescue similar to that of the savings and loan industry in the 1980s." Regrettably, that's exactly what happened. And the federal government's plan to make innocent people pay for the mistakes of previous government officials was the inevitable cost of careless legislation. In fact, those politicians along with many others are trying to fix the financial crisis by applying the same techniques (taxpayer-backed bailouts) that got us in to the mess in the first place, not a good move on any account.

Regardless of its culpability in the mess, government is off on its spending spree trying to revive the economy through the same kind of intervention that cause the various economic woes we face. But we shouldn't become complacent in this government explosion and we shouldn't accept it as the way it has to be from now on. As Executive Vice President of the Cato Institute, David Boaz says, "it is important that the recent emergency measures be recognized as just that: emergency—if not panic—measures and not long-term policy." In fact, these measures can't be honestly considered as long-term policy in the first place. The amount of borrowing and spending that the federal government is doing cannot be sustained and will result in an implosion of the country if it continues for very long.

I'm an optimist and I think that policymakers will eventually realize their wayward direction and right the course, or, more probably, American citizens will realize the root of the problem and elect people who will do the right thing in their stead. In the mean time, there are ways that we can take advantage of the current system and that just might help redirect this aimless and sinking ship.

Part Two
The Techniques

"I'm proud to pay taxes in the United States; the only thing is, I could be just as proud for half the money."
- Arthur Godfrey

"When there's a single thief, it's robbery. When there are a thousand thieves, it's taxation."
- Vanya Cohen

Fight the Fed's Whoopee Cushion

"When I was your age," my grandpa used to squeal, "I would walk to school barefoot in the snow….uphill….both ways. And when I got out of school, I would run to the store and buy an entire turkey for five cents!" Well, my grandpa was apt to exaggerate, especially when it came to finding ways to constantly be walking uphill. But grandpa's complaint about things being cheaper when he was younger was certainly valid. In one of the most pernicious acts of the Federal Reserve (our nemesis from the Introduction of this book), constant inflation of the U.S. dollar became policy in 1913 and ever since, prices of cars, houses, and turkeys have gradually increased as the dollar has steadily lost its value.

You may think that inflation is just the way of the world and it was never different, but that's not the case. Most currencies up until the 20th century were not subject to inflation because they were pinned to something with intrinsic value. For instance, Rome used precious metals (gold and silver coins) as their currency and while the United States used paper money for its first 150 years, it was backed with real gold. Until Franklin Delano Roosevelt's seizure of the shiny stuff in the 1930s (described below), you could actually turn in your US paper money for gold.

However, our currency is no longer backed by gold and that means that the Fed can increase and decrease the amount of money there is at will. Need more cash in the economy? No problem, we'll just print some more. Prices getting too high? No problem, we'll just take some money out of circulation. The Fed has forced what is called a fiat currency system on us—money that exists because an authority declares it to be so, not because of intrinsic value (like precious metal).

The intention behind a fiat system is to give the Fed the ability to adjust the money supply in order to stabilize the economy but it also allows the federal government to recklessly spend trillions upon trillions of green stuff on new bailouts because when Congress needs money to pay for pork barrel politics and they don't want to borrow from China anymore, they can just print more money. The result is that the Fed is inflating our currency like a giant Whoopee Cushion and consequently turning your cash into Monopoly money. In fact, your money lost about 35% of its value from mid-2008 to early 2009—a shocking figure!

The Fed justifies the production of new money by saying that the more people are working, the more wealth there is and thus, we require more dollars to reflect all that new wealth. Without more printed money, the argument continues, there would be deflation and goods and services would actually be worth *less* in dollars over time. But if the Fed really just wanted to reflect the new wealth, they should print only enough money to make turkeys cost roughly the same over time (zero inflation), but the official Fed policy under Alan Greenspan and what looks to

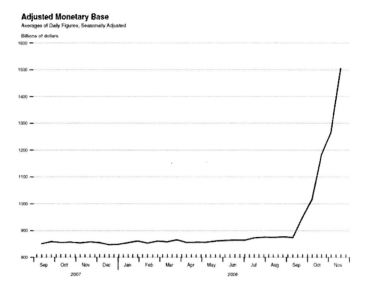

Figure 6. The Fed has injected an unprecedented amount of new artificial money into the economy, inflating the currency at astounding rates.

continue with Ben Bernanke is an inflation target of around three to four percent.

So, the Fed prints more money all the time. It then lends it to banks, which get the privilege of utilizing the full value of the new money. The banks then lend the money to other lending institutions and those lending institutions lend it to big businesses that, in turn, lend it to other businesses or spend it on supplies and employment. The suppliers then get the money and pay their employees and only when those employees go out to dinner or pay their rent is the new money fully incorporated into the economy. But by the time the cash gets down to the lowest rung on the ladder (the common worker), the dollar has lost its value by however much the Fed has increased the money supply.

Seen in this light, inflation is a subtle "tax" that reduces the value of your money year after year. But this subtle tax isn't universal—it affects the bottom rung of the financial ladder (the low- to middle-income workers) more so than the top rung (the government and big banks that get access to the new money first). Since the big banks get to spend the money before it has been fully integrated into the economy, that new money is worth the same as the old money. But by the time it gets down to Joe Worker, the money has been diluted and the tax is in full effect.

This form of taxation is insidious and hard to quantify and as a result, most Americans are unaware of what they are losing in this scenario. But the losses are real and substantial. If Joe Worker has $10,000 invested in a retirement portfolio and earns $1,000 in a year on those investments, he may think that he earned 10 percent. Unfortunately, Joe didn't take into account inflation (generally about 3 percent) and his real earnings only amounted to 7 percent in real wealth. The $11,000 he has at the end of the year is only really worth about $10,670 ($11,000 − $330) because that's how much spending power Joe Worker has after a year's worth of inflation. In other words, if you're making under 3 percent on an investment, you're pretty much breaking even or possibly losing wealth, even if the dollar amount of your investment increases over time. How about that for a *new* deal? More like a raw deal. Inflation is bad; so bad in fact, it led President Ronald Reagan to declare, "Inflation is as violent as a mugger, as frightening as an armed robber and as deadly as a hit man."

Luckily, we're not left to deal with inflation helplessly; there are a couple ways to capitalize on this situation. My brother likes to joke that the best investment nowadays is a new car (which loses about 20 percent of its value when you drive it off the lot—traditionally one of the worst investments you could make), but that's not one of the ways to get around inflation that I'm recommending here. As you'll see, there are some conventional and unconventional ways to get around the inflation tax and start taking advantage of the government that is trying to take advantage of you.

Barter Charter

One solution to this chaotic economic situation is bartering. One of the lost arts of economics is the concept of bartering—trading goods or services for other goods or services without the intermediary of currency. Of course, this practice fell out of favor long ago with the advent of money. Once people could store their wealth in little gold coins with Caesar's mug on them and could buy, not just bear skin or the ceramic pot that other members in their clan could offer, but wine from the Tigris Valley and spices from India. Since Roman times, currency has become even more ubiquitous and bartering is seen as an ancient relic or seen only occurring between primitive hunter/gatherer societies and maybe on Christmas morning.

But bartering is a lost art and one that needs to be revived—especially in trying economic times like these. The main reason is that times have changed since people were selling their oxen or gladiator services for some coin and today's economy is different even from the one we had a hundred years ago.

First off, it appears that a lot of people today have more time than money—a perfect scenario for bartering since money isn't part of the equation. Second, by trading goods or services between each other, you can avoid the possibility of losing value in your cash received when you sell a product or service. Third, transactions outside of the federalized currency system reduce demand for the dollar and thus decrease the need for inflation. Fourth, while the dreaded IRS requires you to claim the barter amount on a 1099-B, the value is up to you to claim—something I find impossibly subjective, but very befitting the IRS. Fifth, technology has given us the ability to find people who want what we have and have what we want. Websites like www.craigslist.org are full of bartering opportunities.

I've already begun a trade for some fine (but very inexpensive, mind you) woodwork furniture and bathroom remodeling. With technology and networking as advanced as it is, it's likely that you already know someone that can provide that fresh dining room paint job or produce a new website for you in exchange for your homemade trinkets or gyroscopes.

The Golden Ticket

The Treasury can print money indiscriminately now because of one factor: the currency is not tied to any precious metal. Throughout the history of America, there were multiple currencies (even thousands) and the main U.S. currency (the dollar) was tied to gold (and other precious metals at times). This made the dollar stable, reliable, and therefore desirable. The Fed changed all that in 1913, established a lone currency in the U.S., and took it off of the gold standard. What's worse, to ensure their monopoly on the currency, FDR signed Executive Order 6102 (often called the Gold Confiscation) in 1933, "forbidding the Hoarding of Gold Coin, Gold Bullion, and Gold Certificates." Gerald Ford reversed this policy in 1974 so that we can now own gold bullion. However, according to the federal government, contracts are unenforceable if participants use gold as a form of currency as opposed to simply a commodity.

The result of all this is that we can now own gold and invest in gold, but the U.S. dollar is not tied to gold in any way. So, while the Fed continues to inflate the U.S. dollar, gold reserves remain relatively stable and thus, gold prices continue to rise. That is why many financial advisors consider gold the safe haven for your money—it is generally inflation-proof.

Of course, gold isn't going to double in price based on a good quarter; it's a roughly static commodity and not Microsoft. But with the way the Fed is printing money and the way the stock market has been tanking, gold could be your best bet to increase the dollars in your portfolio.

There are a number of ways you can invest in gold. One is by buying gold bullion through vendors like www.monex.com/prods/gold.html. You can also get government-approved gold and other precious metals through their approved list: www.monex.com/prods/gold.html. Another way to invest in gold is through gold Exchange Traded Funds (tickers: GLD, IAU), which attempt to reflect the price of gold in its share price, or gold-related stocks like Newmont Mining (ticker: NEM), Placer Dome (PDG), or Barrick Gold (ABX).

Acknowledging the Fed's policy to inflate the currency and how that acts as a silent tax, I invented a way to get around that: a website in which people can transfer their wealth into gold and pay people with the precious metal (or the electronic representation of it). While researching this book, I've come to learn that my idea wasn't original and there are well-established companies that are already providing this service. A list of these "digital gold currencies" can be found here: http://en.wikipedia.org/wiki/Digital_gold_currency.

Getting TIPSy

If beating inflation alone through gold isn't appealing enough to you, you may want to consider a Treasury bond that is protected against inflation. A Treasury Inflation-Protected Security (TIPS) is a security that inflates and deflates along with the Consumer Price Index (CPI). In other words, when the TIPS matures, the principle is paid either as it was when the security was purchased or adjusted to match inflation (whichever is greater).

Interest on TIPS is paid twice annually at a fixed rate and applied to the adjusted principle so that the interest earned is relative to inflation as well. The interest rates on TIPS are fairly low (rates around the time of this writing were at 1.375 for a 3-year note and 2.75 for a 10-year note), but the added protection against inflation could make for a profitable investment. Most advisors will say that a well-diversified portfolio must have some inflation-protected securities in it.

You can purchase TIPS through the government at TreasuryDirect.gov or through an ETF like iShares Barclays TIPS Bond Fund (ticker: TIP).

Refinance Or Don't

Stocks have been falling like some crazy base jumper off a Patagonian cliff and banks are going out of business like no one's business. This economy is officially ugly. One of the results is the federal government has tried to infuse the economy with more cash so that people start lending again and business as usual can resume. How does the government do this? The Fed injects more money into the economy by lowering interest rates for the funds it loans to other banks (more on this below). When rates are lower, banks tend to loan more and that generally results in more spending ("Hey, I would only be paying 1% on the loan for that sweet Escapade, I'll buy it!"). More spending usually means more demand for stuff around the country and that means more jobs.

That's the plan at least, and that's why the Federal Funds Rate stands at 0-0.25% at the time of this writing. The only thing it could do with that rate to encourage more spending is to make it negative—pay banks to take money out. At any rate, money is dirt-cheap right now, and, while that doesn't directly mean that other financial rates are going to follow suit, some have. In particular, mortgage rates, while fending off the Fed rate's steady decline for a while, have finally come down and are poised to keep going down to reflect the cheap money out there. At the time of this writing, the national average on a 30-year mortgage rate was under 5.2 percent—a historically miniscule number—and I know of a couple people financing their homes at much lower rates. Some are saying that rates are at "all time lows" and to be sure, since the '70s, we haven't seen anything like 5 percent (1980 showed us mortgage rates of nearly 20 percent, for instance).

So, it's clear that now is a great time to refinance and secure a rate of 5 percent for thirty years. However, there's another great option; you can wait. The big thing five to ten years ago was the adjustable rate mortgage (ARM) which gave the borrower a ridiculously low rate for three, five, or seven years, then switched to a variable rate, which was presumably going to be higher. This was a dangerous mortgage to have when the rates were high and people owed more on their loan than the house was worth (which is what happed in the housing crunch), but rates are very low right now. Many variable rates are based on U.S. Treasury bond yields such as the 6-month Treasury yield, which sits at around 0.4 at the time of this writing. For example, my variable loan is based on the 1-year Treasury Yield Rate. The Lender tacks on a predetermined margin rate to the index rate (based on the Treasury yield) and viola, you have your new variable rate.

While the 5 percent interest rates on a 30-year mortgage are extremely tempting, the variable rate might be lower. You may want to pass up on that refinance if your adjustable rate mortgage is about to adjust. If that ARM is based on the basement-dwelling Treasury yields, you will probably get a much better yield with the variable rate. And it appears that the Fed rate isn't going anywhere anytime soon — those yields will be low for quite a while as the Fed continues to try to stimulate borrowing and spending. You could ride out the wave of low interest rates for a while, save a couple thousand dollars and refinance when it seems like the rates are going back up. Of course, this takes a crystal ball and unless you feel comfortable with predictions of such a chaotic indicator, it may be wise to refinance while you know you can get an outstanding rate.

The culprit in this system is benign — the Fed just wants us to spend more money, so the Fed makes money cheap. But if you don't take advantage of it, you gain a disadvantage to the banks and financial bigwigs who are taking advantage of the current economic times. This opportunity comes perhaps only once in a lifetime—maybe not even that often. It's time to take advantage of it!

Here's what you do to see if this technique can apply to you and help you take advantage of the people who are trying to take advantage of you:

1. Call your mortgage bank and ask them how they determine the adjustable rate.

2. Check the current treasury yields at www.ustreas.gov/offices/domestic-finance/debt-management/interest-rate/yield.shtml

3. Compare the new rate with your old rate and the average current 30-year fixed mortgage rates at: www.bankrate.com/.

It may make sense to spend a couple thousand dollars to refinance, but if your adjusted rate beats the current refinance rate or even your old pre-adjusted rate, you may be better off sticking with the variable rate.

Modify Your Loan

One thing we kept hearing during the so-called debate on the pork-filled stimulus package of February 2009 was that there had to be more support for mortgage borrowers! If it's clear that the mortgage industry collapse created the entire financial mess as most economists are claiming now, I'm not sure why Congress didn't focus solely on that issue to resolve the economic crisis, but as it stands, only part of the stimulus package includes a "Homeowner Affordability and Stability Plan"—to the tune of $75 billion. The idea is to help homeowners keep their homes that they irrationally bought with the help of the federal government (as described in the Introduction). The government will do this by artificially lowering their interest rates and thus their monthly payments, making homeownership manageable for that economic demographic.

I know, I know. This sounds an awful lot like the type of government intrusion that got us in to the mess in the first place and I don't recommend, as economist Walter Williams said, sending in the arsonist to stop the fire. My point with this technique isn't to fix the economy, though; my point is to help people take advantage of the people who are trying to take advantage of them. In this case, the government is trying to take advantage of us by intruding into the market (again) and forcing lower interest rates on homes that are in high risk of foreclosure. The money that lenders lose on these modified loans will have to come from somewhere. In this case $50 billion of it will come from the already-in-debt federal government and the remaining $25 billion will come from Fannie Mae and Freddie Mac, both of which are in government receivership, which means the government will be footing the bill there too. As Lyle Grimley, a former Federal Reserve Governor said, "It's all coming from taxpayers pockets one way or the other." On top of that, the plan forces lending companies to compensate for an additional portion of the reduced interest rate. But those lenders aren't going to simply take a loss for that; they're going to make up for it by increasing the rates elsewhere—on customers who aren't taking advantage of the government plan.

It seems to me, then, that with this brilliant government scheme, you're either taking advantage of it or you're being taken advantage of. The very least you should do is check to see if you can be part of the former group.

According to the U.S. Treasury, if you are suffering from the falling home prices, you can partake in the upside-down pyramid scheme the government calls stimulus. According to the Treasury worksheet the government plans to:

Provide the Opportunity for Up to 4 to 5 Million Responsible Homeowners Expected to Refinance: Mortgage rates are currently at historically low levels, providing homeowners with the opportunity to reduce their monthly payments by refinancing. But under current rules, most families who owe more than 80 percent of the value of their homes have a difficult time securing refinancing. (For example, if a borrower's home was worth $200,000, he or she would have limited refinancing options if he or she owed more than $160,000.) Yet millions of responsible homeowners who put money down and made their mortgage payments on time have – through no fault of their own – seen the value of their homes drop low enough to make them unable to access these lower rates. As a result, the Obama Administration is announcing a new program that will provide the opportunity for 4 to 5 million responsible homeowners who took out conforming loans owned or guaranteed by Freddie Mac and Fannie Mae to refinance through the two institutions over time.

Reducing Monthly Payments: For many families, a low-cost refinancing could reduce mortgage payments by thousands of dollars per year. For example, consider a family that took a 30-year fixed rate mortgage of $207,000 with an interest rate of 6.50% on a house worth $260,000 at the time. Today, that family has $200,000 remaining on their mortgage, but the value of that home has fallen 15 percent to $221,000 – making them ineligible for today's low interest rates that generally require the borrower to have 20 percent home equity. Under this refinancing plan, that family could refinance to a rate near 5.16% – reducing their annual payments by over $2,300.

Notice that the government institutions that pretty much led us all into this mess (Fannie Mae and Freddie Mac) get benefits that responsible companies (that aren't in receivership) don't get. If you're in bed with the GSEs, then you've got the golden ticket; otherwise, this technique is a little more difficult. Those who don't have loans associated with Fannie or Freddie must watch the dropping home values of our neighborhood and wait until the loan value is greater than 80 percent of the value of the house in order to qualify for the special loans. Given that many borrowers failed to put 20 percent down when they bought their home, this applies to millions of households. With continuing to plummet housing prices, the number of at-risk homeowners continues to grow.

If you are close to an at-risk mortgage situation, there are a few things to keep in mind. While it's important to keep paying your mortgage in order to maintain good credit, it's vital to not pay any more than you are required by the terms of your loan. If you want to take advantage of a lower interest rate thanks to your neighbors, pay the absolute minimum (principle and interest with applicable escrow fees) and nothing more. You want your principle to remain as high as possible as the value continues to dip. As prices drop, your loan-to-value percentage may end up at or above 80 percent in which case, you will qualify for the government-mandated low rates.

If the low interest rate seems just too good to pass up, but your loan-to-value percentage is well below the 80 percent limit, there is a considerably more reckless way to take advantage of the plan: put a Lexus on your credit card. That's right, the government wants to help those who can't help themselves, so the lower interest rate on homes will be granted to those who have high total debt levels. This means if you have a lot of credit card debt (i.e. you had recently purchased $20,000 worth of llamas or a $40,000 cruise around the world), the lower rate is yours! Of course, to take advantage of this loophole, the bureaucrats will want something from you—they require you to go to credit counseling to qualify for the loan:

> ***Special Provisions for Families with High Total Debt Levels:*** Borrowers with high total debt qualify, but only if they agree to enter HUD-certified consumer debt counseling. Specifically, homeowners with total "back end" debt (which includes not only housing debt, but other debt including car loans and credit card debt) equal to 55% or more of their

income will be required to agree to enter a counseling program as a condition for a modification.

For more information, visit the Treasury at www.ustreas.gov.

Downsize Your Life

Times are tough and people are losing their jobs. Companies are cutting back and people are doing without. It's times like these, then, that seem opportune to do a little spring-cleaning of one's life. Perhaps you should be doing a little cutting back as well—maybe it's time to downsize your life. Are you just letting the newspaper pile up on your porch without even picking one up now and then? Are you letting your gym membership card collect dust? Do you really need that subscription to *Hannah Montana Monthly*?

I'm sure there are things in each reader's life that they can downsize and save a little money and a that small amount here there can really add up. Here are some techniques that I've thought up or learn about from friends that will help you keep more of the green stuff that's getting sparser and sparser.

Pay It Forward

I was spending less than anyone I knew on my phone bill each month, but it still hit $60 some months and was consistently over $50 (so much for the $39.99 a month plan I thought I had signed up for). Despite my mysteriously growing phone bill, I had been doing most of my telephoning online through Skype (a nice program that lets you talk to anyone in the world for free as long as they also have a Skype account, and to any cell phone or landline for a small annual fee). So, I did the math and decided to switch from a typical post-pay phone plan to a pre-paid system. With the new system, I provide an initial deposit to the phone company and each call I make costs me $0.10 a minute (each day I use the phone costs an additional $1). This would start to add up if I was on the phone all day every day, but I'm not, and so I make the $50 I previously spent in one month stretch to four or five months now. The total savings for switching to a pre-paid plan comes to about $400 a year.

Disclaimer: the process to switch to a pre-paid phone from a post-pay plan was not easy. Since I wanted to keep my number and the process was usually reversed (people usually go from pre-paid to post-paid), it took some time and effort to accomplish the task. But after a few weeks of customer service tennis (in which I was the ball), I had my new cost-effective system in place. During the process, and using some of the consumer techniques I outlined in the first *How to Take Advantage of the People Who Are Trying to Take Advantage of You* book, I ended up with a new phone, which has most of the basic features but nothing elaborate. The new phone cost $15 and for the life of me I can't figure out how something so technologically sophisticated can be so inexpensive (with no government subsidies mind you), but that's the case.

If you have multiple cell phones, a home phone, and an Internet phone, you may also want to consider dumping one or more of them to save money. You're not Lebron James' agent and you probably don't need so many redundant ways for the world to get in touch with you, so do yourself and your wallet a favor and hung it up.

Hug a Tree

No, this isn't some Arbor Day dedication, this is a money saver. Eating out is expensive and buying healthy food from the grocery store isn't much cheaper. So, if you eat a particular fruit or vegetable a lot, I recommend that you plant a fruit tree (or a couple dozen) or invest in a small garden for vegetables and/or herbs. Real farmers or gardeners will talk endlessly about the benefits of working on the land and actually producing something of your own to help your subsistence, but there are also great financial benefits to such an endeavor. A fruit-bearing Meyer lemon tree can run you upwards of $75 dollars, but if you enjoy a glass of fresh-squeezed lemon juice every once in a while, the investment will pay off easily within the first year. An avocado tree will cost you $60, but each avocado it bears is like a tasty green dividend that saves you $2 a pop. The savings really start to multiply when you consider an herb garden. Some herbs from the store cost just as much to consume once as they would to plant and keep indefinitely. A critic would say, well, just remove those items from your diet if they're too expensive, but if you have a favorite fruit or seasoning, planting some of your own might just be the best way to save a little cashola.

If you do own your own garden, you'll likely find that the fruit it bears is more than you and your family can consume. If that's the case, find friends who also keep gardens, and use the bartering technique described earlier to expand your homegrown menu. Half a dozen home farmers could equal a whole produce department. Oh, and, don't forget to include those home wine and chocolate makers in this enterprise as well.

Free Movie Night

I enjoy a good Pixar movie just as much as the next person—in fact, I would say that movies in general (not just hilarious animated ones) are my preferred form of entertainment. That being the case, then, I made sure to include the pay movie channels when I had the cable installed; I had a subscription with the online movie rental company Netflix; and I purchased movies from iTunes every once in a while. But not only was I paying for those entertaining venues, I was paying for my local library down the street (through taxes) and wasn't using it. So, I decided to give up the commercial avenues of home entertainment and go with just the library, which, it turns out, has a pretty large selection of flicks that satisfy my film fix just nicely. While the library doesn't have everything, the selection is decent and already paid for (coerced as it was).

I'm able to save nearly $100 a month on entertainment costs alone by strolling to the library instead of paying up for cable and online movie distributors. *The Incredibles* never looked so entertaining!

Store No More

Most people get a storage facility with the intention of keeping it for a short time only, which is how they can justify the $100 monthly fee. But the convenience of having that extra storage space is too hard to give up when it's time to move out, that's why many people end up keeping their storage space for extended periods of time, sometimes lasting up to five or even ten years. When you do the math, it may be time to close the door on the storage place and pocket the Benjamin each month. And if you can't keep all of it in your house or apartment, sell it and make some more money.

Do It Yourself

When my toilet was leaking recently, I could have called the plumber and asked him to take a $60 look at the pipes, but I chose to look into it making the fixes myself. Like farming and gardening mentioned above, rewards for do it yourself (DIY) fixes go beyond saving money (knowledge of the inner workings of one's house and a visceral sense of accomplishment come to mind as rewards well worth the time and effort). But, this is a book about bucks, so, let's talk turkey. The plumber would have cost $30 an hour at least and he would have overcharged for the parts needed to complete the task. On the other hand, it took me 15 minutes on the Internet and a $5 trip to The Home Depot to determine what was wrong and get the materials need for the common fixer. Household DIY jobs don't come along every day (fortunately), but when they do arise, it's nice to know that you can pretty much do most fixes in your home yourself. So save yourself some moolah and hit up websites like www.doityourself.com or www.ehow.com to get started.

The good thing is that, even in this ugly economy, we aren't nearly as bad off as those poor souls in the 1930s, who had to worry about finding their next meal. Our economy may contract as much as it did back then percentage-wise, but financially and technologically, we're still light years ahead of the first Great Depressioners, so that there's absolutely no chance that large sections of the population will be starving next year. We don't have to cut back on the food that we eat; all we need to do to thrive in this economy is make a few adjustments and do some things that we'll enjoy doing anyway.

Invest In Your Future

The stock market lost a lot of its value in 2008—so much that the year has the dishonor of containing the worst 1-year drop in stocks to kick off a recession (about a 40 percent decline compared to a roughly 30 percent drop in the year following the 1929 stock market crash). But as we've seen with our concise history of economic depressions earlier, the economy usually bounces back, even after really depressing depressions. Despite government intrusion and against all likelihood, somewhere in the middle of a contraction, stocks always find a way to come back.

And when stocks do come back, an interesting aspect of trading makes that comeback extremely valuable. Let's say a stock started 2008 at $100 a share and lost 40 percent of its value that year. If the stock were rebounded in 2009 to get back to $100 a share, it will have gained 67 percent of its value that year. It seems like a magic trick—down 40 percent but up 67 percent—where did the other 27 percent come from?

The trick really isn't a trick, it just involves common fractions. $40 of $100 is 40 percent, but $40 of $60 is 67 percent. Of course, if you have one position of any given stock and take the round trip down and back, you'll end up with the same amount at the end of the investment roller coaster. However, if you got out of the coaster car on the descent and got back in at the bottom, you would have been able to capitalize on the volatility in the market—something all great investors from John Pierpont Morgan to Warren Buffet have done. Also, even if you kept your position (and didn't sell it to realize the loss for tax purposes), you can still capitalize on the market by doubling up while the stocks are cheap. This is what is called beating the market (a goal often eschewed by economists because they seem to think it can't be done). Sell high and buy low.

And stocks are indeed low. At the time of this writing, the Dow was near a 6-year low and the Price to Earnings ratio (PE) for the S&P 500 was just under the historical norm of about 18. It's impossible to determine exactly when the market will rebound and when it rebounds, if it is rebounding for good, but it's almost guaranteed that the market will eventually rebound. After the economic depression of 1893, the Dow Jones Industrial Average more than doubled in the rebound; then after losing over 40 percent of its value in the 1907 crisis, the Dow nearly doubled again from 1908-09. Another plunge in the Dow in 1914 following the installation of the Federal Reserve System was met with another doubling in 1915-16.

The Great Depression was another story altogether however. With the massive intrusion into the free markets, Roosevelt's seizure of gold, and unbearable regulation, the market did not react as soon as it could have otherwise. The Dow Jones Industrial Average lost 90 percent of its value in the four years following the stock market crash of 1929 (good thing we had the Federal Reserve to prevent economic collapses like that right?), but it didn't get back to its previous high for quite some time. Still, the average did more than quadruple in value from mid-1932 to 1937. Investing in 1932, no matter what you lost in 1929 would have been a profitable venture.

Since the first Great Depression, we've had plunges of 30 percent (1962), 40 percent (1973-74), 30 percent (1987), 20 percent (1998), 30 percent (2000-03), and the 40 percent plus decline of 2008-09. In each case prior to this last one, the stock market has rebounded within the following five years and in each case, the Dow surpassed the previous high. Granted, it probably seemed like the markets wouldn't ever recover in each of those cases, but they did. And each retraction probably seemed irreconcilably devastating (as does the current one). But good investors knew that they weren't. Yes, this market is statistically worse than all of the declines since the first Great Depression, but even in the 1930s, stocks came back with a vengeance. They will come back with a vengeance this time too.

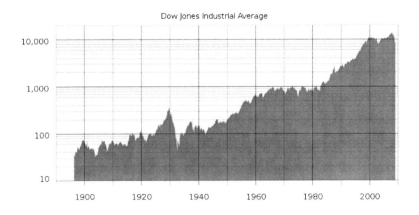

Figure 7. The Dow Jones Industrial Average has always found a way to recover from major declines.

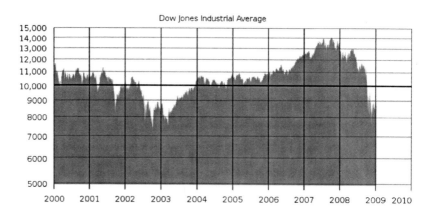

Figure 8. While the decline in stocks is more substantial this time, they should recover as usual.

The trick is how to know when to start investing so that you aren't part of the decline, but instead you are part of the recovery. I'm not a fortune teller and I think that anyone who tells you that they know exactly when the markets will start a real comeback are selling snake oil. But one thing is clear, investors fear losing their money more than they fear missing out on potential gains. This mentality leads to one generality every investor can make about the market: stock markets drop very quickly but rise gradually. After the crash in 1929, stocks recovered, but took 23 years to get back to where they were in September 1929. In 1962, it took six months to plummet 30 percent and a year and a half to get back to where it was prior to that. In the seventies, it took two years for the Dow to fall 40 percent, and eight years to get back to where it was before. The 1987 crash took two months to occur and over a year to recover from. The 1998 crash is the only exception to the rule (the market rebounded in the same amount of time it took to decline), but this could be accounted for the fact that the correction in the late nineties was relatively minor and wasn't accompanied by an economic recession.

There have not been any studies on this quick-decline-slow-recovery phenomenon, but the facts are available in any market chart.

Of course, this applies to the market as a whole as opposed to individual stocks. An individual stock can skyrocket on news that it just sold a million widgets in a day, then slowly decline based on the news that the widgets are faulty and a competitor just came out with better widgets and so on. On a more general plane, the Dow Jones and other indexes reflect an overall confidence in the market, which shows the pattern described here. You can take advantage of this down market by buying low and holding on during the long haul upward.

So the question is, what should you buy?

The Market as a Whole

The question remains, then, what should you buy? A quick answer to that is that you should buy the market as a whole. It's a guaranteed win in the long run (which may turn into a double marathon the more the government interferes with the recovery), and eventually, investing in the market as a whole through diverse mutual funds will bring solid returns. Of course, with little risk, there is also little gain. Another option is to double down on the market. There are Exchange Traded Funds (ETFs) that capitalize in such a way that they aim to reflect twice the return of a given sector or market—the fund manager uses leverage to double the gains or losses. For instance, the ETF company, ProShares, offers a series of funds called ultra funds that reflect twice the return of a given portfolio. The Ultra S&P500 fund (ticker: SSO), "seeks daily investment results, before fees and expenses, that correspond to twice (200 percent) the daily performance of the S&P 500® Index." This could be a great way to capitalize on a down market as it rebounds, as it accelerates the trip back by two times. Many estimates have the S&P 500® rebounding over the next few years back to where it was in 2007. That would mean an 80 percent gain for the market and roughly double that for the Ultra S&P fund SSO.

Short Toyota

With the Big Three U.S. automakers getting a richly undeserving bailout from the U.S. taxpayer, they can continue to exist. And, since they're now subsidized, their competition may suffer as a result. Toyota, which recently became the world's largest automaker (surpassing GM), is the main competitor of the Detroit companies and will suffer as the American carmakers get financial support by the government. With the bailout, the Big Three will be able to continue their broken ways and perhaps even gain market share by cutting prices (GM already is offering employee pricing for its cars), so it may be wise to sell Toyota (ticker: TM) and maybe even buy GM in the short term. You will want to reverse course when the bailout wears out and buy Toyota in a few years while shorting the heck out of the Big Three. That is, of course, assuming that the bailout runs out, which doesn't look likely to happen any time soon as GM, Ford, and Chrysler continue to beg for more money from the you, the taxpayer.

Buy Wally World

One of the major companies that haven't lost over 40 percent of its value since the downturn began in 2008 is Wal-Mart. The world's largest retailer actually reported the strongest sales figures in its history for the fourth quarter of 2008, while the rest of the retail world was tucking tail and running for the hills. Wal-Mart must have something figured out because even well respected discounters Costco and Target have taken a dive since September of 2008. Both have lost nearly half of their value in the same time Wal-Mart has just given up 20 percent. No labor unions and continual drive to cut costs has given Wal-Mart the edge and while it has seen a small dip in price, it looks like the bellwether will be able to come out of the recession in excellent form. It's true that you want to invest in under priced stocks, but you also want to put your money into companies that have proven that they can succeed. Wal-Mart is just one of those companies.

Buy Green

The stimulus package of early 2009 had numerous earmarks and pork projects designated for environmental projects within the government including $3.7 billion to conduct "green" renovations on military bases, $3.4 billion for fossil energy research (possibly including an earmark for FutureGen), $5.1 billion for environmental cleanup around military bases, $5.5 billion for "green" federal buildings, $300 million for "green" cars for federal employees, $600 million for the EPA Superfund environmental cleanup program, and $200 million to clean up leaking underground storage tanks. All of this green action will require green companies to either produce the materials needed to supply the projects and that means investment opportunities.

It's true that alternative energy companies have seen a spike in the early half of the first decade in the 21st century and a subsequent sell off, but the rebound may happen soon and it may outpace stocks in general. Besides the specific mention of FutureGen above, there is no clear indication of what companies will benefit from these green initiatives (as a matter of fact, there is no clear definition of what "green" even means). Still, you get the idea that the Democratic-lead federal government wants to brand the economy with a green tint and there will be money to be made. www.altenergystocks.com offers a rundown on popular alternative energy companies as does www.renewableenergystocks.com/. Both are good resources for finding short-term moneymakers in a green economy. Maybe money does grow on trees after all!

Short What You Downsized

Chances are that if you are cutting certain things out of your economic diet, other people are doing the same. So, it may make sense to sell stocks of the companies that you aren't doing business with any more because of the economy. If you shop at Value Village instead of Urban Outfitters nowadays, it may be time to dump URBN. If the newspaper doesn't make the cut in your streamlined life, maybe you should sell your Gannett shares (ticker: GCI). Of course, this parallel between personal financial choices and stock price doesn't always ring true. I put my Netflix account on hold in late 2008 and the stock promptly gained 40 percent. Still, your personal choices are a good indication of what everyone's doing and if you've stop supporting the company, it might be time to sell the stock as well.

Grab a Grant

All over the Internet, I'm seeing ads for financial services claiming that Obama gave someone $12,000! Or, "I paid $2.99 and got $23,984 from the government!" Whether it is to pay for bills, get out of debt, or go save the Chiricahua Leopard frog, these advertisers claim that there are government grants to be had for every American and you too could be basking in the warm sunshine of no-strings-attached government funds.

Well, I haven't taken these marketers up on their wild offers (the claims remind me of some outrageous diet claims that promise you'll lose five pounds each week (which, by the way, would be equivalent to 10 marathons-worth of energy)! But the concept does deserve some investigation. The government does provide grants consistently—upwards of $150 billion a year—but much of the money goes to states or government agencies, not to individuals who need help paying their bills or even those who want to start a business.

Billions of dollars in grant money is available to non-government agencies—money you could rightly be entitled to as a US citizen—but there are a few steps to take in order to receive the cash. And, contrary to popular opinion, the money you get from the government (ultimately your money in the first place) is not given without restriction. The grantee is required to fulfill his end of the bargain or face economic sanctions, or in the case of theft or fraud, jail time or other penalties.

Now that we have the disclaimers out of the way, let's see how you can get in on the action and start taking advantage of the government that is trying to take advantage of you.

1. Find a Grant that Fits Your Goals.

There are two websites that the federal government has created to insure transparency while offering billions of your dollars back to you in unbalanced ways: http://www.grants.gov/ and http://www.cfda.gov/. At the time of this writing, the cfda.gov (Catalog of Federal Domestic Service) site was under construction, but the grants.gov site provided a clear, simple list of grants available for application. From the home page, click on the link "New Opportunities This Week" to access all the new grants offered. You'll find grants for anything from creative writing to, yes, saving the Chiricahua Leopard Frog. Many of these grants are designated for government agencies, but there are quite a few that are available to individuals or non-public organizations as noted within each grant description.

2. Establish Yourself as a Qualified Applicant.

Many of the grants have one prominent requirement and that is that the organization must be a state government, a municipality, or a non-profit charity. Since you probably can't or don't want to start your own state government or municipality, that leaves you with becoming a non-profit charity, which isn't as difficult as it may sound. First, you should either incorporate or establish articles of association (which consists of describing the intent of your organization and listing the members). Then, apply for non-profit status through the federal government with the IRS form f1023 (found at www.irs.gov/pub/irs-pdf/f1023.pdf). Applying for a 503(c)(3) exemption will cost $300 for most organizations, but there are a number of benefits including not having to pay taxes on income made through the organization and the ability to apply for many government grants.

You can also receive grants to get education and start a small business, but those situations may not fit your situation.

3. Apply for the Grant

To apply for the grant, return to grants.gov and go to the designated grant synopsis. On that page, you'll see a link for 'Application', which will direct you to the electronic application for your specified grant. After you've completed your application, the process will generally take about 1-6 months and you should have your decision, perhaps along with the associate grant.

The federal grant system is by no means as easy as some advertisers are claiming it to be. And no, Obama isn't personally giving you money, but there is money to be had for things you may already be doing. Government officials are taking advantage of your work ethic by forcing you to pay taxes for these grants; you might as well be returning the favor!

4. Spend the Money

Federal grant money does not have to be paid back and certainly doesn't accrue interest while it is being used, but there are restrictions. You can't, for instance, use the money from your grant to buy a lifetime supply of Häagen Dazs ice cream. The grant must be used for the direct purpose that is laid out in the grant application. If you are granted the grant to save the Chiricahua Leopard frog, it had better not go extinct while you spend your grant on rich and creamy frozen desserts.

Capitalize on Unemployment Insurance (That's Why We Have It!)

A friend and I were recently lamenting over the state of the US dollar. Since the inception of the Federal Reserve, the value of the dollar has consistently shrunk, mainly because the Treasury prints more and more money for the same economy (more dollars for the same value equals less value for each dollar in the equation).

But since the "worst financial disaster since the Depression" began to show up on the news media radar in late 2007 and, consequently, since the federal government has been desperately trying to correct the disaster by injecting more cash in the system, the Treasury has been printing money like there's no tomorrow.

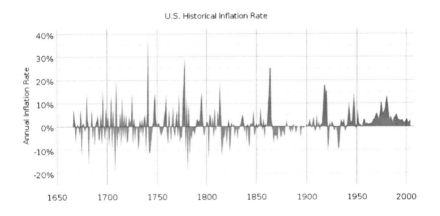

Figure 8. Inflation has been the norm since the first Great Depression, devaluing your money and making your work worth less and less over time.

One estimate puts the amount of money printed since last year at 70 percent of the original amount, which means that your cash has taken a serious dive in value. Not only has your 401k gone down in value because of the stock market crash, the amount that it's actually worth compared to other currencies is much less than that. That 401k might be looking a little like an 1k pretty soon, all thanks to Alan Greenspan and his successor at the Fed, Ben Bernanke.

So, what can you do about it? Well, until we voters can get our act together and terminate the Fed, there's not much we can do about it. My friend seemed to think there is one way to take advantage of the system in the mean time, however.

Since inflation takes some time to trickle down to the working class (inflated currencies benefit the big banks who receive the money first, and end up harming the working class who get the additional money last), my friend figures that working while the money proliferates through the system is actually counter productive. His plan is to just sit back and collect Unemployment Insurance for the full year allotted, then resume working when the inflation has been substantially integrated into the economy. It's like selling the stock (his labor) high and then buying it back at a low price.

This may sound crazy, but it really makes a lot of sense. First, because the Fed's money infusion addiction will ultimately decrease the value of our money, it doesn't make sense to work extra hard and accumulate the cash that will continue to lose value until they stop printing at ludicrous rates. Second, my friend is getting the full Unemployment Insurance allotment of $450 a week based on his last job, which more than covers his expenses (basic and frivolous). And third, he needn't feel guilty about collecting money that has already essentially come out of his paycheck. He's paid for this broken system, so he should be able to benefit from it, or so the logic goes.

I'm certainly not one to promote welfare—if it came to a vote tomorrow about whether to continue the program, I would vote to terminate Unemployment Insurance. But the moral problem isn't when people collect the cash; the moral problem is when the government takes the cash by coercion in the first place. It's not wrong to receive money, it's wrong to unjustly take it. I don't think government should be in the business of paying people not to work. Then again, I don't think the government should be in charge of building roads, yet I'm not going to stop driving on the ones that they have already built.

So, I recommend that everyone take Unemployment Insurance until the Fed stops printing money like they made the board game Monopoly. Perhaps only then will the entire country wake up to the damage that the Fed does to this economy.

Here's what you do:

1. Get Laid Off

It's not hard to do in this economy. Every week we hear on new layoffs form this company or that company. In fact, I think that every single person I know has been laid off at least once in the past year. Sometimes companies seek out people willing to take severance and offer to be laid off and, other times, some hapless employees just get the call whether they want it or not. If your company is hurting financially, talk to your boss and see if you can be officially laid off. Quitting and being fired won't help because they don't meet the requirement of wanting work where none is available.

2. Sign Up for Unemployment Insurance Benefits

Unemployment is controlled through each state and each state is different. Most have clear websites (see below for a list of the website URLs) and easy-to-follow instructions on how to start taking advantage of the unemployment benefits. You will need to input your previous employer information and your salary rates. This is what your benefits will be based on.

One thing to note is that it is a much cleaner process if you don't have any employment at the time of application. A friend of mine applied to receive unemployment after she was laid off from a school she was working at. She still was employed part time with another employer and this caused a lengthy process to establish what her claim was going to be, including an interview by a couple of the nice government workers and others who liked to hang up on her. Another friend of mine applied for unemployment and did not have to go through a phone interview because he proclaimed himself as completely unemployed. Keep in mind that the Unemployment Insurance system, like Social Security and other government welfare programs, is antiquated and practically obsolete since it was designed for a past economy (e.g., before the Internet and the more volatile job market). The notion of freelance work doesn't really jibe with the old-school structure of UI.

Once you fill out the application, you will receive an employment package in the mail and soon after you will receive your first weekly (or biweekly) unemployment form.

Here is the list of unemployment benefits websites by state:

Alabama - http://dir.alabama.gov/citizen/
Alaska - http://www.labor.state.ak.us/esd_unemployment_insurance/home.htm
Arizona - https://egov.azdes.gov/CMSInternet/main.aspx?menu=234&id=2550
Arkansas - http://www.state.ar.us/esd/WorkersUnempBenefits/ADWS_Workerunempben.htm
California - http://www.edd.ca.gov/Unemployment/default.htm
Colorado - http://www.coworkforce.com/uib/
Connecticut - https://iic.ctdol.state.ct.us/welcome.aspx
Delaware - http://www.delawareworks.com/Unemployment/welcome.shtml

D.C. - http://www.does.dc.gov/does/cwp/view,a,1232,q,537855,doesNav,%7C32062%7C.asp

Florida - http://www.floridajobs.org/unemployment/index.html

Georgia - http://www.dol.state.ga.us/js/unemployment_benefits_individuals.htm

Hawaii - http://www.hawaii.gov/labor/ui/index.shtml

Idaho - http://labor.idaho.gov/dnn/UnemploymentInsurance/UIBenefits/tabid/681/Default.aspx

Illinois - http://www.ides.state.il.us/individual/

Indiana - http://www.in.gov/dwd/2418.htm

Iowa - http://www.iowaworkforce.org/ui/file1.htm

Kansas - https://www.uibenefits.dol.ks.gov/

Kentucky - https://uiclaims.des.ky.gov/ebenefit/

Louisiana - http://www.laworks.net/UnemploymentInsurance/UI_Claimants.asp

Maine - http://www.maine.gov/labor/unemployment/benefits.html

Maryland - http://www.dllr.state.md.us/employment/unemployment.html

Massachusetts - http://www.detma.org/DETUI.htm

Michigan - http://www.michigan.gov/uia

Minnesota - http://www.uimn.org/ui/index.htm

Mississippi - http://www.mdes.ms.gov/wps/portal/%21ut/p/kcxml/04_Sj9SPykssy0xPLMnMz0vMAfIjzeMN4p299a-NyUtMTkyv1Q_P0w3ITKzJzM6tSU_Qj9KPMgPKWLiCdIJaj-fiRUwNcjPzdVP0g_WN9bP0C_ICerysfE0REAVIQS4Q%21%21/delta/base64xml/L0lJSk03dWlDU1lKSi9vQXd3QUFBWW-dBQ0VJUWhDRUVJaEZLQSEvNEZHZ2RZbktKM-EZSb1hmckNHODAvN18wX0NLLzM%21?PC_7_0_CK_MESCCommand=UnEmployment#null

Missouri - http://www.dolir.mo.gov/es/

Montana - http://uid.dli.mt.gov/

Nebraska - http://www.dol.state.ne.us/nwd/center.cfm?PRICAT=1&SUBCAT=1B

Nevada - http://detr.state.nv.us/uiben/uiben_uiben.htm

New Hampshire - http://www.nh.gov/nhes/

New Jersey - http://lwd.dol.state.nj.us/labor/ui/ui_index.html

New Mexico - http://www.unemploymentoffice.net/State_resources/New%20Mexico.htm
New York - https://ui.labor.state.ny.us/UBC/home.do
North Carolina - http://www.ncesc.com/
North Dakota - http://www.state.nd.us/jsnd/
Ohio - http://jfs.ohio.gov/ouc/bucb/
Oklahoma - http://www.oesc.state.ok.us/UI/UI-claimant-info.shtm
Oregon - http://findit.emp.state.or.us/benefits/
Pennsylvania - http://www.dli.state.pa.us/landi/cwp/view.asp?a=355&q=235210
Rhode Island - http://www.dlt.ri.gov/ui/
South Carolina - http://dol.sd.gov/ui/default.aspx
South Dakota - http://dol.sd.gov/ui/default.aspx
Tennessee - http://www.tennesseeanytime.org/unemployment.html
Texas - http://www.twc.state.tx.us/customers/jsemp/jsempsub2.html
Utah - http://jobs.utah.gov/ui/
Vermont - http://www.labor.vermont.gov/
Virginia - http://www.vec.state.va.us/index_ui.cfm?loc=unins&info=insur
Washington - http://www.esd.wa.gov/uibenefits/index.php
West Virginia - http://www.wvbep.org/bep/uc/
Wisconsin - http://www.dwd.state.wi.us/ui/
Wyoming - http://wydoe.state.wy.us/doe.asp?ID=316

For more information, check out the United States Department of Labor's website factsheet about unemployment at http://workforcesecurity.doleta.gov/unemploy/aboutui.asp.

3. Cash Your Check

Within a few weeks you should receive your first check accompanied by the form for a continued claim (some states require a buffer period of one week that negates your first week of unemployment insurance). The money is taxable (which is almost as bizarre as taxing taxes), but it's yours to do whatever you want with. It should be quite enough to live off of and perhaps—as one of my friends is doing—enough to live off of and save.

Some people that I know who are collecting unemployment say that it is not necessary to look for a job or show proof of that search while collecting unemployment, but it wouldn't hurt. The most you have to do is put down the employer name, address, and date of application for each week you claim unemployment. It's not that difficult and gets you ready for when you actually need to get off your keister and go get a job.

You can continue this process for up to 26 weeks and after that point, you can apply for an extension of another 26 weeks. If you're not completely drained of all motivation to do something with your life after the first 26 weeks, why not take the government up on another couple thousand? After all, you've already paid for it—either it came directly out of your paycheck or your employer paid for it and gave you a lower wage to make up the difference. You might as well take advantage of this program; millions of other Americans already are.

Avoid It Like the Plague

Mark Harris Getty is one of the grandsons of oil tycoon Jean Paul Getty and he created the photo archive website Getty Images, which provides some of the best stock photo services in the industry. John Dorrance III is an heir to the Campbell Soup fortune. Ted Arison is the founder of the successful Carnival Cruise Lines. J. Mark Mobius is an international money manager. What do these people have in common with hundreds of others (besides being filthy rich)? They all renounced their U.S. citizenship and moved to countries that had more lenient tax laws. In other words, they are rich and they didn't feel like the federal government was a very good investment for their hard-earned cash.

They were avoiding taxes like the plague, and who could blame them? Taxes kill wealth like a fiduciary black death.

Some may call these people tax cheats or may condemn them for tax evasion, but what they did was completely legal at the time and absolutely ethical (some would just call it good business). The billionaires mentioned above were just taking advantage of a tax loophole that was open for everyone. The federal government taxes income of U.S. sources of income up to 35 percent and then taxes the remaining wealth 45 percent (to be changed to 55 percent in 2011) when you die. However, these taxes only apply to U.S. citizens; the billionaires mentioned above naturally wanted to avoid coughing up so many millions of dollars, so they bugged out. Some live in Europe; some live in the Caribbean; all are keeping more of their money and passing more of it on to their children than if they had stayed a U.S. citizen.

For most people, renouncing their U.S. citizenship would not save them much money and, in fact, would be a pretty silly thing to do because most people don't have billions of dollars to save in the process and because of all the places in the world, the U.S. isn't such a bad place to belong to. And it wouldn't matter even if you wanted to leave now because after so many billionaires caught the next boat to the Caribbean in the '90s on, the government enacted an "exit" tax on all the wealth gained while in the country, which made people who were renouncing their citizenship to fork over 35% of their wealth.

Still, it seems like the extremely wealthy get all the breaks; that's why it wasn't so shocking when the second-richest person in the world, Warren Buffett announced that he paid a lower tax rate than his secretary. He said in an interview that his office tallied up all the payroll and income taxes for their employees and Buffett's rate came to 17.7 percent of his income and his employee's tax rate came to 32.9 percent. I mentioned a similar conundrum in the first *How To Take Advantage* book: billionaire Ross Perot pays less of a percentage of his income in taxes than does the average American. Perot paid 8.5 percent to Uncle Sam while the average American paid 12.9 percent. So, not only do wealthy people get to live it up in fancy jets and million dollar mansions, they also pay less to the government. How in the world is that possible? How in the world can it be considered fair?

It's fair because the federal government says it is. They've set up a tax system that is so convoluted and full of so many incomprehensible loopholes that the average American worker has very little choice but to pay a set percentage of their income (as determined by Congress) whereas billionaires with or without big floppy ears and squeaky Texan accents have the resources and opportunities to make money that will be taxed at a lower rate. The difference is how you make your money. For instance, Warren Buffett's employees and the average American all make their money as salaried employees and are taxed by the graduated income tax (10 percent for people making up to $8,025 and up to 35 percent for people making more than $357,700). But Buffett's salary is just $100,000; he makes the rest of his money from capital gains via security sales (which has a maximum of 15 percent tax).

Obviously, the system that taxes wealthy people a smaller percentage than poorer people leaves a lot to be desired. It just goes to show how distorted and antiquated the leviathan we call the tax code has gotten over the course of its existence. If you're a working-class American who makes money as an employee, you're paying more to the federal government. If you're already wealthy and make money off of your money, you pay less. Moreover, as we'll see, there are ways that wealthy people can completely avoid paying taxes altogether—legally—whereas the average worker is stuck paying their income tax and Social Security tax, and Medicare tax, and state income tax that come out of each paycheck.

It doesn't have to be like that. There are ways to level the playing field that anyone can partake in. If you get your income from an employer, you are a bit limited to one technique: itemizing your deductions. But you can also start a business and start reaping the benefits from that. In addition, there are other more unconventional ways of avoiding taxes that apply to those of us who don't receive money from an employer in the traditional sense. You can do it too; you too can take advantage of the government that is trying to take advantage of you—legally and ethically. And you don't even have to renounce your citizenship.

Itemize

Many people who have the ability to deduct from their taxable income at the end of the year in order to get a larger portion of their money back from the government don't bother to do so. They may not know what expenditures they can deduct, or they might not feel like spending the time compiling all their receipts and sorting them when it's tax time. This is understandable. Americans already average 27 hours in completing their tax return every year. At a reasonable $20 an hour, the cost of doing one's taxes is $540 in lost potential income, and that doesn't even include the accounting efforts put forth throughout the year.

If you're not getting back more than $540 in your return (many of us don't), it's not really worth it to be so diligent in making sure the government gets only their share and no more. It makes you wonder if that mentality is what government officials were counting on when they made the process so difficult in the first place. Is it possible that tax-code policy makers envisioned a lazy public who would give the government more money in exchange for more free time? If you're at all cynical about government motives, you may find that question to have an obvious answer. A summary of this process may reinforce the cynicism: 1) Government takes money you've earned before you can even say, "rip off." 2) Government sometimes takes more than you owe. 3) Government puts in place a convoluted refund system that makes it difficult to get back any money that you overpaid throughout the year. 4) Government charges *you* interest if you underpay.

Regardless of the government's motives, many taxpayers don't even bother to get the money that they are owed. Amazingly, in fact, the home mortgage interest deduction goes unclaimed more than half the time for those who qualify for it. With the home mortgage interest rate, we're talking about a potential tax savings of thousands of dollars, yet, a few hours in early April is more valuable to most homeowners. In this case, IRS officials really have done amazing things to take advantage of us taxpayers.

If everyone automatically received the deductions available through the tax code, the system would be more just. However, these deductions are being looked over the people who need them most (you and me). It irks me to think that some wealthy people are intentionally avoiding their tax obligations, while other less well-off citizens are blindly donating more than their fair share to the government by not taking advantage of those deductions. However, I do understand that justice alone may not entice many readers and that money might make for a more compelling reason to act on these special tax code gems. You can make a major impact on your income if you itemize your deductions and resist the urge to take the effortless standard deduction. The reason for this is that there are seemingly endless possible deductions. The IRS categorizes deductions into these groups:

1. Medical and dental expenses
2. State and local income taxes, or sales tax
3. Real estate and personal property taxes
4. Home mortgage and investment interest
5. Charitable contributions
6. Casualty and theft losses
7. Job expenses
8. Miscellaneous deductions

Those may seem pretty vague and general, though. A longer list of deductions can be found in the back of this book, but I'll go over some deductions that may help you to lower your taxable income and some that may surprise you. You can deduct medical and dental expenses if they are over 7.5% of your gross adjusted income for the year in addition to popular deductions like charitable donations and state and local taxes (federal taxes cannot be deducted, incidentally). If someone has stolen your antique clock, you can deduct it; or, if a mad antelope has escaped from the zoo and rammed through your front door, subsequently getting trapped in your house and destroying everything you have (casualty losses must be sudden and unusual), you can deduct the expense involved. You can deduct work-related schooling costs and the gas mileage required to get to that school. If you are a schoolteacher, you can deduct supplies that you have purchased, and, if you're an Armed Forces Reservist, you can deduct travel expenses. Additionally, you can deduct union dues or dues to professional organizations that help you to do your work.

Those are fairly obvious deductions, but some people have taken the often-vague deduction system to the extreme, trying to deduct some bizarre things. Some of these deductions were audited and subsequently rejected by the IRS, but others make sense and can find a place in the legal realm of tax reporting. While claiming your dog as a dependent is unlawful, a taxpayer in Dallas deducted the cost of his guard dog's food as a security expense. On that note, you can also deduct the depreciation of livestock or other animals, but incidentally, only if they're used for breeding.

A Spanish teacher, also in Texas, was able to write off his television and cable expenses for the betterment of his occupation because of the Spanish-language channels. Deductions for improvements in occupational skills can even go beyond what most of us think as just. Chesty Morgan, a Detroit area stripper, tried to deduct her breast implants as a medical expense and was brought into a tax court, where a judge reprimanded her. He also did her a big favor and allowed her to deduct the expense of her enlarged bosom as a business expense. Interestingly enough, if Chesty had deducted her new floatation devices as a medical expense, she would only have been able to write them off if their cost had exceeded 7.5% of her adjusted gross income; whereas, if they are considered a business expense, their cost only needs to surpass 2% of her income—quite a difference.

The general idea here is that Chesty and our Texan friends were trying to capitalize on the deductions of the Federal Tax Code. They, like most of us, make money, and the government is allowed to take some of that income, thanks to the representatives around in 1913. However, when you purchase any of the diverse and bizarre collection of items that have been approved by the IRS as tax-deductible, your taxable income is reduced by that amount. The ultimate goal of this Ad-in technique is to reduce your taxable income by acknowledging these purchases on your income tax return and reduce your tax liability, preferably to zero.

Start a Business

There are 15 million people who own businesses that are considered Sole Proprietorships, according to the IRS, and that number is growing. Those 15 million people are smart entrepreneurs who are quite possibly taking advantage of some major benefits to owning a business, particularly when they're the only person in the business. Whether you start a business to provide you with your entire income or to earn some extra money here and there, you can count on two major benefits to doing business as a sole proprietor and also some drawbacks. If you are financially stable, you can stand to profit from this popular type of endeavor. If don't think you can start a business or you don't want any additional hassles, perhaps you should consider starting one based on a hobby or other interest. Starting a business is simple, educational, usually very fun, and can help you take advantage of an overly complex tax code.

The first major benefit to starting your own business is that, while you do business as a sole proprietor, you avoid a double tax on the revenue that you bring in. What is a double tax? You might ask. A corporation pays taxes on the money it makes and the money it pays to its employees. Those employees, then, pay taxes on their income as well—this is the second time an income tax would be applied to the same income (a double tax). When someone owns their own business, or has a sole proprietorship like a lemonade stand, the government views him and his business as one entity, making the double tax impossible. When he makes money on each cup of lemonade, he doesn't have to pay the corporate tax, just his income tax.

You can look at it this way: when you spend a dollar at Wal-Mart, you are giving about 40-60% to the government, but if you spend a dollar at Joe Schmoe's Lemonade Stand, you are giving 10-35% to the government. The difference is widened even more when you consider additional corporate taxes that are levied on companies' profits. Joe Schmoe pays taxes just once on his revenue.

But, you might say, if I don't have a business in the first place, then I don't have to worry about the double tax, because I don't really notice it. This may be true because income tax is only taken out of your income dollars once, but the fact that your company is spending taxes on top of paying you your salary certainly affects what you make. When an employer hires someone with a $50,000 salary, the employer must consider the taxes (income, Social Security, Medicare) that he must pay in addition to salary. These taxes can add up, and they restrict the amount an employer can offer his or her employees. If your company paid you as a contractor, you would get your full pay, and the company would take it as a loss and wouldn't have to pay income tax or any other tax on it. The company could pay you $65,000 for the same work you were doing at $50,000 and make money.

The other key benefit to opening a sole proprietorship is the ability for sole proprietors to count their business expenses against other income, for example, income from a traditional day job. That is to say that you can deduct the new lawn mower purchased for your weekend landscaping company from the money you received from your IT job. This is where the stickiness comes into play with regard to all the tax deductions and write-offs. The IRS is very clear with how we can deduct certain expenditures from our income, but there are a wide variety of things you could be deducting if you only had the knowledge of what deductions were possible. Well, now you have that knowledge: http://www.irs.gov/businesses/small/article/0,,id=109807,00.html. The IRS website is surprisingly extremely helpful in sorting out what business expenses can be deducted and under which circumstances.

Looking over the website may convince you that it's not worth all the effort to sort out the appropriate deductions, but believe me, it is. If you have a business selling rare Italian gel pens with plastic propellers at the ends, and you conduct a business dinner with a customer to explain why he should buy 50 million of them, you can deduct that dinner's expense from your pen-selling income or the income from your day job. In fact, you can deduct just about anything business-related as long as it meets two criteria: the expense has to be ordinary and necessary. In other words the expense has to be common in your industry, and it has to be helpful to your business. Buying a $3,000 pair of shoes to impress your customers probably won't pass as a legitimate business expense in the auto industry, but, if you're reasonable, the government will be more than happy to provide you with tax deductions galore in promoting your business.

Much of what you're already spending now *without* a business can actually be seen as a deduction in the eyes of the IRS. Thus, starting a business can automatically help you save money on your tax liability. And it doesn't take much to get started. In many cases, you'll have to file for a business license, and, if you're going to do business in a name other than your own, you have to file for a Fictitious Business Name with the local municipality. But those are generally small and hassle-free fees when you consider the amount of benefits you may gain from this Ad-in technique.

These are the kinds of things you can deduct when you own your own business:

- Filling up your gas tank to visit a client in Podunk
- Dinner at Claim Jumper for you and your best clients
- Skybox tickets at the stadium for you and 10 business associates
- Tickets to a charity gala (if all the proceeds go to the charity)
- The new computer that you do your accounting on
- A portion of your home mortgage or rent (if you have a specific home office designated)
- Medical insurance premiums

The main trick is to start living your life with the intent to save money on nearly everything you do. A sole proprietorship is a great start to making your taxable income next to nothing, and it's actually promoted by the IRS.

If you're convinced that starting your own business would be a good idea, you may still be wondering what you could sell or do with your own business. Here are some ideas:

As mentioned before, you could contract with your current company to do the job you already do, saving your employer money while being able to write off your commuting expenses, your home-office expenses, and the laptop you just bought to do your work on.

Another option is to start a business doing something that you find enjoyable, such as a hobby. If you like gardening and know some people that could use your services, you can start a small business as a gardener. The IRS distinguishes businesses from hobbies by the expectation to make money. If you do not expect to make money, you can still receive deductions, but there is a limit to the amount you can deduct. Also, if you don't create a business out of your hobby, you can't deduct losses on your hobby from your primary income.

The IRS suggests that you consider the following factors when deciding whether your hobby can be considered a business:

1. You carry on the activity in a business-like manner
2. The time and effort you put into the activity indicate you intend to make it profitable
3. You depend on income from the activity for your livelihood
4. Your losses are due to circumstances beyond your control (or are normal in the start-up phase of your type of business)
5. You change your methods of operation in an attempt to improve profitability
6. You, or your advisors, have the knowledge needed to carry on the activity as a successful business
7. You were successful in making a profit in similar activities in the past
8. The activity makes a profit in some years
9. You can expect to make a future profit from the appreciation of the assets used in the activity.

Other easy-to-start companies to consider are Internet-based companies, which we briefly mentioned before, and consulting — anything from wedding planning to dietary consulting. One self-employed business that I'm particularly familiar with is writing. The tax benefits from all of these are nearly as long as the 3.4 million-page tax code, and they're simple to get started.

There are risks with starting a sole proprietorship business, however, and those risks vary from industry to industry. In a sole proprietorship, since you and your business are indistinguishable, your company's liability is yours as well. If you are driving around in your ice cream truck, which you use to run your company, Jen & Barry's Ice Cream, and you run over little Bobby's foot, his parents might sue. You may have been little Bobby's favorite ice cream maker before the accident, but after the accident, his parents could not only bankrupt your company and take away the truck, they could also take away your personal savings account, your house, and your dinner. The liability doesn't end at the business side when it comes to sole proprietorships, just as the deductions don't end on the business side of your income. You and the business are one entity, and that may cause some tension in certain industries. This is likely why most sole proprietorships are not in high-liability industries. Though it's not impossible, it's unlikely that anyone will sue you and your website that makes money off of advertising click-throughs.

In the early '90s, real estate mogul and recent television star (reality television sex symbol?), Donald Trump, had a series of unfortunate financial setbacks, and his company went bankrupt, as it couldn't keep up with the interest on hundreds of millions of dollars in loans. If Trump's business had a sole proprietorship, Trump himself would have gone bankrupt, but he wasn't personally responsible for his company, and he never had to declare bankruptcy for himself, thus enabling *The Donald* to go on to reclaim billion-dollar status. If you are in a risky industry and don't want to jeopardize your life savings or your family's well being, you should consider starting an S-Corporation or a Limited Liability Company. These business structures allow you to operate your company as your own without assuming the full risk. To learn more about these company structures, pay a visit to the website for your state's friendly Secretary of State. The site should be complete with lengthy explanations of all different business structures and what it takes to get started in business with one.

Move to Greener Pastures

There are fewer and fewer differences between states with regard to laws and government interference, partly because the lines between the federal government and the states are blurring more and more, and partly because most states agree on how their residents should be governed. One thing is still vastly different from state to state and that's taxation. Some states have bucked the federal trend since 1913 and kept their grubby little hands off of its residents' income while others have followed suit with Uncle Sam. The result is that many people move to these states if they make a lot of income or if they live off a fixed income as in the case of retired folks.

There are nine states that don't have a state income tax: Alaska,

U.S. States with No Income Tax

Alaska – has a state corporate income tax.
Florida – has a state corporate income tax. Once had tax on "intangible personal property" held on the first day of the year (stocks, bonds, mutual funds, money market funds, etc.) but was abolished at the start of 2007. The Florida Constitution explicitly prohibits a personal income tax. Nevada has no personal or corporate income tax. Nevada gets most of its revenue from gambling taxes.
New Hampshire – has an Interest and Dividends Tax of 5%, and a Business Profits Tax of 8.5%.
South Dakota – has a state corporate income tax on financial institutions.
Tennessee – does have tax on income (at a 6% rate) received from stocks and bonds not taxed ad valorem (Tenn Const Art II, §28). The Tennessee Supreme Court has held that a personal income tax is unconstitutional (Evans v. McCabe).
Texas – in May 2006, passed a franchise tax on businesses (sole proprietorships and some partnerships are exempt). The Texas Constitution places severe restrictions on passage of a personal income tax and use of its proceeds.
Washington – has a Business and Occupation Tax (B&O) on gross receipts, applied to "almost all businesses located or doing business in Washington." It varies from 0.138% for splitting dried peas to 1.6% for bigtime gambling.
Wyoming

Florida, Nevada, New Hampshire, South Dakota, Texas, Tennessee, Washington, and Wyoming. These states have become destinations for the hard working and the hardly working (as in the case of the retirees that flock to Florida) and that may have an impact on the ability of these states to escape much of the damage incurred during recessions (after all, innovative and hard workers create wealth and don't sap it). A study conducted in 2008 showed that half of the top ten recession-proof cities in the nation were located in the nine states without income tax—a remarkable figure. Note: the income tax isn't the only factor in beating the recession, however, as Florida and Nevada have been crushed in the current recession (mostly attributed to their real estate foreclosure problems).

You may be inseparably attached to your life in New Jersey or Iowa, but if saving an extra 2 to 9 percent off of your income tax bill is appealing to you (about $10,000 for an average middle-class family), you may want to consider greener pastures in Texas or Tennessee.

Take It Off Shore

If moving to an income-tax-free state and saving up to 9 percent on your income doesn't quite do it for you (you want to avoid the other 35 percent income tax, plus the social security tax and Medicare tax, etc.), perhaps doing business in another country is the way to go. You've no doubt heard of tax shelters and havens and it may have piqued your interest despite the negative light they are often portrayed in. The fact is that using these tax havens can be legal and, as it might be said, just good business. I'm going to show you how to take the next step and legally make income without being taxed.

The purpose in this book is not to hide monies earned in the United States for the purpose of deceiving the Internal Revenue Service (IRS), which is an illegal practice called tax evasion, but to actually earn the money in another country. An example of tax evasion is if Warren

Buffett pays his secretary $1,000 in cash for cleaning his windshield and his secretary doesn't claim the income on his tax return. It was income earned in the United States by a U.S. person and thus, should be taxed accordingly. Evasion is not what I'm suggesting here.

What I am suggesting is to establish a corporation under a separate jurisdiction in order to make money not as a U.S. person, but as an international corporation. This is a legal practice called tax avoidance.

Like each state, each individual country has its own set of taxes that discourage certain types of behavior (by taxing them) and promotes others (by not taxing them or giving them tax credits). The U.S. federal government, for instance, taxes income relatively heavily (up to 35 percent) and does not tax consumption (sales tax is administered by the states); it could be said, then, that the U.S. discourages working and production and promotes consumption. On the other hand, there are countries that don't tax income or they don't tax income with that originates in another country (foreign source). When you combine this no-tax policy (or a low-tax policy) with secure banking, you get what is called an optimum tax haven.

There are a number of countries that fit the ideal profile for a tax haven and they include The Cayman Islands, The Bahamas, Cook Islands (none of which tax foreign-source income), and Switzerland, Austria, and Liechtenstein (which have low tax rates). Each haven has its strengths and weaknesses; for instance, the Caribbean countries are ideal in their proximity to the United States, but have worse banking secrecy policies than the European countries.

Because each tax haven has different laws that affect the ideal setup, we will focus on two countries with which to operate: The Cayman Islands (for corporate set up) and Switzerland (for international banking purposes).

The first step in legally avoiding taxes is to establish a company in a foreign tax haven. For our purposes we will be describing this process for The Cayman Islands (or Cayman), which is one of the most popular jurisdictions for corporations seeking an escape from high-tax countries. Cayman is ideal because of its solid history of English common law and tax neutrality dating back to its settlement in the 1700s. Cayman's government welcomes pretty much anyone to start a company within the country and will not tax the company as long as it does its business mainly outside of the country. If your business sold coconuts on the beach on Grand Cayman, the government would tax you; but if your business made money through investments in the U.S. or Hong Kong, that income would not be taxed. The open tax policy in the Cayman Islands is why there are over 40,000 companies in the small island nation of 100 square miles—nearly a company for each of its permanent residents.

To set up a company in The Cayman Islands, you will need two directors (one of which can serve as a secretary) and a purpose for the business besides tax avoidance. In this example, the company will be set up as an investment firm, though it could be as simple as the marketing of wildebeests on the Serengeti or a website for how to avoid taxes in high-tax countries. The company will be designated as what the Cayman government terms an Exempted Limited Partnership. The Cayman government will not tax your business as long as the company's activities are carried out in other jurisdictions; they get their revenue by charging initial setup fees (CI$410 for companies with capital under CI$42,000 up to CI$1,968 for companies with capital over CI$1.64 million (the Cayman dollar is pegged to the U.S. dollar at $1 = CI$1.20).

After the initial setup, the only action required by Cayman is for each company to produce a basic annual report that claims nothing has changed with regard to the Memorandum of Association and that the company's business was conducted mainly outside of The Cayman Islands.

Once you've established your company offshore, it's time to get to work. While in Grand Cayman, you'll want to take a jaunt down

Selected Tax Havens

Andorra - No personal income tax.
Anguilla - A British Overseas Territory and offshore banking center
The Bahamas - Levies neither personal income nor capital gains tax, nor are there inheritance taxes.
Barbados - A 'Low-tax regime' not 'Tax haven'. - The government of Barbados sent off a high level note to members of the United States Congress recently in protest of the label "Tax Haven" stating it has the potential to undermine or override the Barbados/United States double taxation agreement.
Belize - No capital gains tax.
Bermuda - Does not levy income tax on foreign earnings, and allows foreign companies to incorporate there under an "exempt" status. Exempt companies may not hold real estate in Bermuda or trade there, nor may they be involved in banking, insurance, assurance, reinsurance, fund management or similar business, such as investment advice, without a license. The island also maintains a stable, clean reputation in the business world. At present, there are no benefits for individuals. In fact, for a non-Bermudian to own a house on the island, they would have to pay a minimum of $15,000 a year in land tax alone.
Bosnia and Herzegovina - 10% corporate income tax, 10% income tax, 10% capital gain tax.
British Virgin Islands: The 2000 KPMG report to the United Kingdom government indicated that the British Virgin Islands was the domicile for approximately 41% of the world's offshore companies, making it by some distance the largest offshore jurisdiction in the world by volume of incorporations. The British Virgin Islands has, so far, avoided the scandals which have tainted less well regulated offshore jurisdictions.
Cayman Islands - No capital gains tax.
Hong Kong - Tax rates are low (17%) enough that it can be considered a tax haven. Hong Kong does not levy tax on capital gain as well.
Ireland - Did not tax the foreign income of authors and artists until 2006. Corporation tax is only 10% or 12.5%. Income not remitted to Ireland by Irish residents not-domiciled in either Ireland or the UK can escape taxation Ireland.
The Isle of Man - Does not charge corporation tax, capital gains tax, inheritance tax or wealth tax. Personal income tax is levied at 10-18% on the world-

wide income of Isle of Man residents, up to a maximum tax liability of £100,000. Banking income tax is levied on the profits of Isle of Man based banks at 10%.

Macedonia - Corporate taxes 10%, income taxes 10%, tax on reinvestment profit 0%

Monaco - Does not levy a personal income tax.

Nauru - No taxes. Only tax in country is an airport departure tax.

New Zealand - Does not tax foreign income derived by NZ trusts settled by foreigners of which foreign residents are the beneficiaries. Nor does it tax the foreign income of new residents for four years. No capital gains tax.

Norfolk Island - No personal income tax.

Panama - 'Offshore' entities are not prohibited from carrying on business activities in Panama, other than banks with International or Representation Licenses (see Offshore Business Sectors) but will be taxed on income arising from domestic trading, and will need to segregate such trading in their accounts.

Switzerland - A tax haven for foreigners who become resident after negotiating the amount of their income subject to taxation with the canton in which they intend to live. Typically taxable income is assumed to be five times the accommodation rental paid. Vaud is the most popular canton for this scheme. For businesses, the canton of Zug is popular, with over 6000 holding companies.

Turks and Caicos Islands - The attraction of the Exempt Company lies in a combination of its tax exempt status and minimal disclosure and administrative requirements.

United Kingdom - A tax haven for UK residents of foreign domicile who pay a flat levy of £30,000 on their non-UK income.

United States - Some states, particularly Delaware, offer incentives for businesses to locate there. Many banks and other financial companies are domiciled in the state of Delaware even though Delaware is one of the smallest states in the United States. US-banks also offer a wide range of offshore private banking to south american customers.

United States Virgin Islands - Offers a 90% exemption from U.S. income taxes and 100% exemption from all other taxes and customs duties to certain qualified taxpayers.

to 227 Elgin Avenue to the UBS House to set up an offshore account with one of the largest banks in the world. You'll need a bank account to take care of your finances for your business and UBS is ideal for our purposes. UBS is a diversified global financial services company based in Switzerland, and is one of the, "best capitalized banks in the world," according to the chairman of the Swiss National Bank. Since UBS is so well diversified, it can be the one-stop shop for your brand new financial investment company, and its anchor in the strong banking secrecy tradition of Switzerland makes it ideal for the type of safe tax avoidance you're interested in.

You may be skeptical of this if you read the *New York Times* or other major papers in February of 2009. The claim was that UBS was giving up its secrecy policy at the bequest of the Internal Revenue Service (headline: "A Swiss Bank Is Set to Open Its Secret Files"). But privacy still exists as it always has for people who follow the law. The reported 250-300 names that were turned over to the IRS belonged to people who broke the law in order to evade taxes. This is not what we're recommending here and one shouldn't be worried about losing anonymity by using UBS as long as one works within the law.

You'll want to set up your account as an offshore account in any of the locales which UBS has an office (from Brazil to Hong Kong) in order to comply with Cayman laws to conduct your business offshore. Once you've opened an account with UBS for your Cayman company, you can operate your business from anywhere with an Internet connection. UBS offers anything from investment funds, structured products, and non-traditional asset classes such as hedge funds (many of which are not available to people in the United States due to regulation) to real estate, commodities and private equity. Since your company is based in a no-tax haven, you will be able to enjoy a tax-free investment environment for your capital and it's completely legal.

You may be asking if we're investing offshore in a Switzerland bank, why do we need to go through Cayman in order to establish a

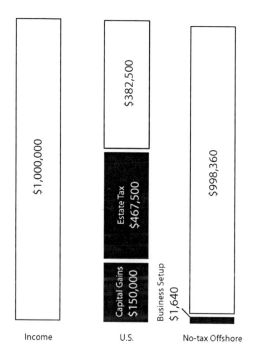

Figure 9. Taxes on production in the United States make Offshore investment very appealing

company offshore? The answer is based in U.S. tax law. If you are a U.S. "person", you will be taxed on any income you make even if it's made offshore (an exclusion of up to $80,000 exists for people who earned that money while living outside of the U.S.). But if you are a Cayman "company," the U.S. doesn't have any legal right to the money earned through that business. Of course, once you pull the assets out of your account and acquire it in the United States, the IRS will count it as income for your U.S. person, which presents a problem.

One way around this is to loan the money from your Cayman company to your U.S. person (loans are not taxable as income). This may raise an eye at the IRS and cause them to shut down the transaction, negating the tax advantage of the offshore company in the first place.

In any case, if you act as the foreign company, you should be able to spend within the United States as a foreign entity without having to suffer the income tax. You will have to open a credit card for your Cayman company and use that for purchases (just as you would use your personal credit card on trips abroad now). You will be able to pay your credit card online from your UBS account and not have to worry about transferring money from your tax haven to yourself.

There are some fairly elaborate websites that are dedicated to tax avoidance and if you're interested in learning more, check out www.escapeartist.com and www.sovereignsociety.com. Of course, if you're planning on doing business offshore, it is highly recommended that you consult a tax professional here in the U.S. and in the tax haven that you plan on establishing a company. If you take precautions, however, you should be able to maintain a stream of income that avoids the devastating taxes Uncle Sam places on its income-earners and start to take advantage of the government that is trying to take advantage of you.

Find a Lasting Solution

While all of the above techniques are solid ways of taking advantage of the government that is trying to take advantage of you and easy-to-follow ways of surviving the Second Great Depression, they are not the best that we can do. In fact, the best way to take advantage of the government is to use the tool that we still have to change the system for good: vote. In order to move this economy to a place where government bailouts aren't required and the only thing people are stimulating are their minds, we must vote for a better government—one that doesn't see it as their job to save us from ourselves and one that doesn't get us into sticky economic situations to support their good intentions.

Luckily for an objective reader, this isn't a political issue. Republicans and Democrats have equally overstepped their bounds in trying to get the economy going through coercion and thus, it can be easily said that a complete overhaul of the federal government is warranted.

There are organizations (listed below) that constantly work for real changes to the federal government that will ensure real, lasting solutions instead of Band-Aid fixes like the bailout and stimulus (read "inflation and devaluation") packages muscled through by Congress that will end up harming us in the long run. The organizations listed below work to spread liberty and justice and are the most immediate way to get on the right side of the issue of economic reform. Get on a mailing list, donate, tell a friend, and vote anyone out of office who doesn't at least try to reduce the size of government!

Here are a list of organizations that promote liberty along with descriptions and charity rating (out of four stars) from CharityNavigator.com:

Cato Institute ★ ★ ★ (www.cato.org)

Founded in 1977, the Cato Institute seeks to broaden the parameters of public policy debate to allow consideration of more options that are consistent with the traditional American principles of limited government, individual liberty, free markets, and peace. Toward that goal, the Institute strives to achieve greater involvement of the intelligent, concerned lay public in questions of policy and the proper role of government. The Cato Institute undertakes an extensive publications program dealing with the complete spectrum of public policy issues. In order to maintain its independence, the Cato Institute accepts no government funding. Cato receives approximately 75 percent of its funding from individual donations, with lesser amounts coming from foundations, corporations, and the sale of publications.

Hillsdale College ★ ★ ★ (www.hillsdale.edu)

Founded in 1844, Hillsdale College is an independent, coeducational, residential, liberal arts college with a student body of about 1,300. Its four-year curriculum leads to the bachelor of arts or bachelor of science degree, and it is accredited by the North Central Association of Colleges and Secondary Schools. Hillsdale's educational mission rests upon two principles: academic excellence and institutional independence. Located in rural southern Michigan, the nearly 200-acre Hillsdale campus includes both modern and historic buildings.

Institute for Justice ★ ★ ★ ★ (www.ij.org)

Founded in 1991, the Institute for Justice (IJ) advances a rule of law under which individuals can control their destinies as free and responsible members of society. IJ litigates to secure economic liberty, school choice, private property rights, freedom of speech and other vital individual liberties and to restore constitutional limits on the power of government. IJ provides legal counsel to inner-city entrepreneurs, because their freedom to shape their own businesses directly affects their freedom to shape their own lives and communities. In addition, IJ trains law students, lawyers, policy activists and grassroots organizers in the tactics of public interest litigation and advocacy for liberty. Through these activities, IJ challenges the ideology of the welfare state and illustrates and extends the benefits of freedom to those whose full enjoyment of liberty is denied by government.

The Heritage Foundation ★ ★ ★ (www.heritage.org)

Founded in 1973, The Heritage Foundation is a research and educational institute, a think tank, whose mission is to formulate and promote conservative public policies based on the principles of free enterprise, limited government, individual freedom, traditional American values, and a strong national defense. The Heritage staff—with years of experience in business, government and on Capitol Hill—doesn't just produce research. They generate solutions consistent with our beliefs and market them to the Congress, the Executive Branch, the news media, and others. Their vision is to build an America where freedom, opportunity, prosperity and civil society flourish.

Acton Institute for the Study of Religion and Liberty ★ ★ ★ ★ (www.acton.org)

Founded in April, 1990, the Acton Institute for the Study of Religion and Liberty is named in honor of John Emerich Edward Dalberg Acton. The mission of the Acton Institute is to promote a free, virtuous, and humane society. This direction recognizes the benefits of a limited government, but also the beneficent consequences of a free market. It embraces an objective framework of moral values, but also recognizes and appreciates the subjective nature of economic value. It views justice as a duty of all to give the one his due but, more importantly, as an individual obligation to serve the common good and not just his own needs and wants. In order to promote a more profound understanding of the coming together of faith and liberty, the Institute involves members of religious, business, and academic spheres in its various seminars, publications, and academic activities.

Atlas Economic Research Foundation ★ ★ ★ ★ (www.atlasusa.org)

Founded in 1981, Atlas Economic Research Foundation's mission is to discover, develop and support intellectual entrepreneurs worldwide who can advance the Atlas vision of a society of free and responsible individuals. At Atlas, we believe that our vision of a free society can be achieved through respect for private property rights, limited government under the rule of law, and the market order. Atlas serves the international market-oriented think tank movement by helping develop independent local think tanks and related programs that advance the ideas of freedom. Today, Atlas supports and works actively with approximately 200 market-oriented think tanks—some from highly developed countries and others from parts of the world where economic freedom is poorly understood.

American Enterprise Institute for Public Policy Research ★ ★ ★ (www.aei.org)

Founded in 1943, the American Enterprise Institute for Public Policy Research (AEI) is a nonpartisan institution dedicated to research and education on issues of government, politics, economics, and social welfare. AEI's purposes are to defend the principles and improve the institutions of American freedom and democratic capitalism - limited government, private enterprise, individual liberty and responsibility, vigilant and effective defense and foreign policies, political accountability, and open debate. Its work is addressed to government officials and legislators, teachers and students, business executives, professionals, journalists, and all citizens interested in a serious understanding of government policy, the economy, and important social and political developments.

Other great organizations dedicated to restoring liberty to Americans:

Campaign for Liberty (www.campaignforliberty.com)

The mission of Campaign for Liberty is to promote and defend the great American principles of individual liberty, constitutional government, sound money, free markets, and a noninterventionist foreign policy, by means of educational and political activity.

End The Fed (www.endthefed.us)

End the Fed! activists believe that the Federal Reserve Bank, through its inflation of the money supply and the distortion of free markets resulting from its intervention, is responsible for the current financial and economic crisis. They also hold that the current round of "bailouts" and federal government nationalization of large segments of the financial sector further inflates the US dollar and disrupts the proper functioning of the markets and will ultimately serve to plunge the nation into an even more severe crisis, quite possibly even into a serious depression.

The John Birch Society (www.jbs.org)

United by a strong belief in personal freedom and limited government, plus a sense of duty, members of The John Birch Society have educated millions of Americans on the appropriate role of government. Using educational and concerted action tools of a wide variety—including local lobbying, distribution of literature, email campaigns, news conferences, petitions, and more—members have played a continuous, pivotal role in halting legislation and federal policies that threaten the independence of our country and our people.

Part Three
Conclusion

"The nation should have a tax system that looks like someone designed it on purpose."
- William Simon

"They who can give up essential liberty to obtain a little temporary safety, deserve neither liberty nor safety."
- Benjamin Franklin

Life is inextricably linked to freedom. The more freedom we have as human beings, the longer we tend to live, as I showed in another book of mine, "Everyone Agrees". In the book, I put together data from the Heritage Foundation and Freedom House on the freest countries around the world and data from the CIA Factbook on the life expectancy of those countries. The results are clearer than the day; the more freedom people have within their country, the longer they live. I'm sure we can all agree that life is good, so the natural conclusion to be made from the data presented below is that liberty is also good—just as good as life itself. This was noted in the prescient quote by Thomas Jefferson, "The God that gave us life gave us liberty at the same time; the hand of force may destroy, but cannot disjoin them."

86 | Surviving the Second Great Depression

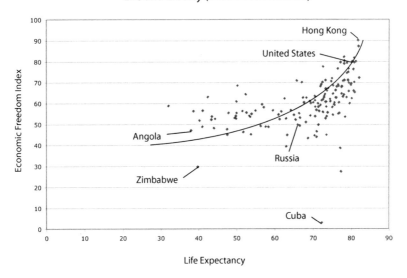

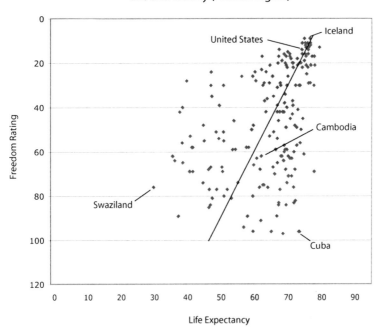

Figure 10-11. Countries with greater liberty (economic and otherwise) tend to have a higher life expectancy.

It is this concept—that life is intertwined with liberty—that creates the strongest repulsion to government intervention in our lives by most people. Yes, the politicians who make up government usually have good intentions, but as some wise man once said, the path to hell is paved with good intentions. Government's only legitimate duty is to protect its people from intentional harm. Government's role is not to ensure a job for everyone and it's not to ensure a chicken in every pot. Government's role is not to make everyone happy in an Orwellian utopia nor is it to make people do something for their own good. And with regard to the economy, government's duty *is* to protect against fraud and injustice and decidedly *not* to ensure a thriving economy all the time.

As we saw earlier, government is powerless to prevent downturns in the economy (especially one as large as we currently have in the U.S.), a fact we've seen validated in the constant efforts to stave off economic recessions since the early 1900s and the subsequent failure of those efforts. Most notable is the recent failure of government to ensure a thriving economy. Officials used the weight of the American taxpayer to boost home ownership (a decidedly good thing) through mandates and regulation (a decidedly bad thing). The result was the housing bubble of the early 21st century and the subsequent bust that brought down the entire financial system with it.

From this description it's clear to see how government intervention may be thoughtful and well intended, but it is usually counter-productive and oftentimes severely detrimental to the society and economy it is supposed to protect. And the knee-jerk impulse after such a massive government failure is to fix the problem with more government intervention, which is what we've seen with the titanic bailouts and stimulus packages that slithered into existence during the recent financial panic.

But if government intervention is seen as an extreme measure to stop the bleeding, it *cannot* be seen as the ultimate solution for our country.

Though government does things productively on one end (increases spending, benefits certain special interests), it requires destruction on the other end (inflation, taxation, regulation, dependence). And while the original duty of a representative government is to protect its people, the result of an intrusionist government is actually the harm of its people. Every law or bailout or regulation or tax the government passes necessarily harms one section of the population even if it benefits another section. And the more our government acts, the less freedom we have. If the charts above are any indication of what that means, the more the government acts, the less we will live to see it happen. What results is a slow self-destruction of the country itself.

Unfortunately, these are the cards we have been dealt. And until enough people realize the repercussions of more government intrusion into our lives in order to change things, we are forced to either look for a new place to live or simply take advantage of the government that is trying to take advantage of us. We can do this completely within the confines of the current system (legally) and work to move toward a more just system all at the same time.

By taking the government up on its numerous offers to "stimulate" the economy and working to sidestep the misguided government policies (like inflation) in other ways, you can capitalize on this system. Finally, you can work toward a lasting solution to economic crises by supporting and getting involved with organizations dedicated to restoring liberty to Americans and by voting pro-government-intrusion politicians out of office. Only then will we finally be able to take advantage of the government that is trying to take advantage of us.

Notes

Introduction

Obama quote: http://www.cnn.com/2008/POLITICS/04/01/dems.oil/index.html.

Prozac Nation

Jay Cooke failure: http://en.wikipedia.org/wiki/Panic_of_1873. Federal expenditures decreased: The World Almanac 2007: 54. Panic of 1893: http://en.wikipedia.org/wiki/Panic_of_1893. U.S. GDP Data: http://www.measuringworth.org/datasets/usgdp/result.php. Schiff quote: http://en.wikipedia.org/wiki/Panic_of_1907. Fed: http://money.howstuffworks.com/fed1.htm. The Great Depression: http://en.wikipedia.org/wiki/Great_Depression. Smoot-Hawley Tariff: http://en.wikipedia.org/wiki/Smoot-Hawley_Tariff_Act. Agricultural Adjustment Administration: Folsom 2009:4, http://www.gjenvick.com/WPA/1935-05-Drought-CurrentFarmImports-Section-01.html, http://en.wikipedia.org/wiki/Agricultural_Adjustment_Act. Higgs quote: Boaz 2009: 7. Recessions after Depression: http://www.bos.frb.org/economic/nerr/rr1999/q3/katz99_3.htm.

The Sky Is Falling…And Falling

Fannie Mae: Driscoll 2008. Community Reinvestment Act: http://en.wikipedia.org/wiki/Community_Reinvestment_Act. MyCommunityMortgage: https://www.efanniemae.com/sf/mortgageproducts/mcm/. Fannie Mae loans: http://online.wsj.com/article/SB122079276849707821.html?mod=hpp_us_whats_news. Nevada GDP: http://en.wikipedia.org/wiki/List_of_U.S._states_by_GDP_(nominal).

Fight the Fed's Whoopee Cushion

Gold seizure: http://www.lewrockwell.com/anderson/anderson154.html. Money supply: http://www.forecasts.org/m1.htm. Regan quote: http://www.npr.org/templates/story/story.php?storyId=94079854.

Refinance or Don't

Since the '70s: http://www.financialmortgagesanramon.com/Mortgage+Rates+Near+All+Time+Lows. Grimley quote: http://money.cnn.com/2009/02/20/news/economy/foreclosure_funds/?postversion=2009022109.

Invest In Your Future

PE Ratio: http://tal.marketgauge.com/dvMGPro/charts/charts.asp?chart=PERATI. Dow history: http://www.djindexes.com/DJIA110/learning-center. WalMart: http://sev.prnewswire.com/retail/20090217/DA7147717022009-1.html, http://www.google.com/finance?q=wmt. Costco, Target: http://www.google.com/finance.

Move to Greener Pastures

U.S. States With No Income Tax: http://en.wikipedia.org/wiki/State_income_tax

Avoid It Like the Plague

Buffett's study: http://flimjo.com/warren-buffetts-tax-rate-is-lower-than-his-receptionists/.

Itemize

Taxes: http://www.pbs.org/wgbh/pages/frontline/shows/tax/view/, http://www.businesstaxrecovery.com/irs_charitable_deductions, http://waysandmeans.house.gov/legacy/fullcomm/107cong/2-5-02/Records/NSA.htm,

Carroll, Robert, Douglas Holtz-Eakin, Mark Rider, and Harvey S. Rosen. "Income Taxes and Entrepreneurs' Use of Labor." Journal of Labor Economics, 18.2 (2000): 324-351. http://www.articleteller.com/Category/Taxes/242, http://www.articleteller.com/Article/Tax-Deductions-for-Your-2005-Hybrid-Automobile/26677, http://www.verticalpulse.com/my_weblog/2006/01/the_american_re.html, http://www.fourmilab.ch/uscode/26usc/, http://www.ustreas.gov/education/fact-sheets/taxes/ustax.html, http://www.irs.gov/newsroom/article/0,,id=110483,00.html, http://www.mises.org/fullstory.aspx?control=1597. Contradictory rates: http://articles.moneycentral.msn.com/Taxes/CutYourTaxes/10bigDeductionsTooManyPeopleMiss.aspx,
Tax trivia: http://www.jacksonhewitt.com/resources_library_tax_trivia.asp, http://www.ustreas.gov/education/fact-sheets/taxes/ustax.html, http://en.wikipedia.org/wiki/Income_tax_in_the_United_States.
History: http://www.taxfoundation.org/taxdata/show/151.html. Deductions: http://skbell1.statesmanblogs.com/tag.aspx?q=itemize, http://online.wsj.com/public/article/SB114234406066997685.html?mod=tff_main_tff_top, http://www.businessknowhow.com/money/50deduct.htm, http://www.irs.gov/taxtopics/tc501.html, http://www.jacksonhewitt.com/resources_library_top50.asp?urlSection=resource, http://www.bankrate.com/brm/itax/news/20020201a.asp?caret=34, http://money.cnn.com/2003/01/29/pf/taxes/q_absurdmoves/index.htm, http://www.leg.state.vt.us/reports/tax/vol2-x02.htm.

Start aBusiness

Mackie-Mason, Jeffrey K., Roger H. Gordon. "How Much Do Taxes Discourage Incorporation?" Journal of Finance, 52.2 (1997): 477-505, http://www.poznaklaw.com/articles/solep.htm, http://www.inc.com/articles/2000/05/19685.html, http://en.wikipedia.org/wiki/Income_tax_in_the_United_States. Business expenses: http://www.irs.gov/businesses/small/article/0,,id=109807,00.html, http://www.smallbiztrends.com/2004/09/best-home-based-businesses_09.html. Corporate taxes:
http://www.csmonitor.com/2005/0314/p17s02-cogn.html.

Take it Offshore

Expatriates: http://www.escapeartist.com/library/article7.htm. Expatriate tax: http://www.pwcias.com/home/eng/globalwatch_us_may2008.html, http://www.palmbeachdailynews.com/biz/content/specialsections/estateplanning/2009/01/11/EP_011109_LauridsenPrice.html. Buffett's tax rate: http://flimjo.com/warren-buffetts-tax-rate-is-lower-than-his-receptionists/. Cayman Islands: http://en.wikipedia.org/wiki/Cayman_islands, http://www.netatty.com/articles/tax.html, http://www.worldlawdirect.com/article/475/Forming_a_corporation_in_the_Cayman_Islands.html, http://caymanlife.wordpress.com/2008/07/22/forming-a-company-in-cayman-islands/. Cayman setup fee: http://www.offshorelegal.org/offshore-corporations/cayman-islands-corporations-incorporation/facts-on-a-cayman-islands-exempt-company.html.
UBS: http://www.ubs.com/, http://www.nytimes.com/2009/02/19/business/worldbusiness/19ubs.html?_r=1&scp=5&sq=UBS&st=cse, http://www.sovereignsociety.com/2009Archives1stHalf/022009SwissBankingSecrecyDeadThinkAgain/tabid/5347/Default.aspx. Selected Tax Havens: http://en.wikipedia.org/wiki/Tax_haven#Examples. Business loan not taxable as income: http://smallbusiness.yahoo.com/r-article-a-1903-m-2-sc-56-is_a_business_loan_taxable_income-i . How rich avoid taxes: http://taxvox.taxpolicycenter.org/blog/_archives/2008/5/29/3719254.html

Conclusion

Jefferson quote: http://jpetrie.myweb.uga.edu/TJ.html.

Bibliography

Boaz, David. "The Return of Big Government." Cato Policy Report Jan. & feb. 2009: 1+.

Driscoll, Gerald P. "End the Mortgage Duopoly." The Wall Street Journal 15 July 2008.

Fels, Rendigs. "The Long-Wave Depression, 1873-97." The Review of Economics and Statistics 31 (1949): 69-73.

Ferriss, Timothy. The 4-Hour Workweek Escape 9-5, Live Anywhere, and Join the New Rich. New York: Crown, 2007.

Folsom, Burton E. "Do We Need A New New Deal." Imprimis 38-1 (Jan. 2009): 4-5.

Goldberg, Jonah. Liberal Fascism The Totalitarian Temptation from Hegel to Whole Foods. New York: Doubleday, 2007.

Morse, Joseph S. How to Take Advantage of the People Who Are Trying to Take Advantage of You: 50 Ways to Capitalize on the System. Ed. Eric Robert Morse. Grand Rapids: CoDe, 2006.

Morse, Joseph SB. How To Take Advantage of the People Who Are Trying To Take Advantage of You Credit Arbitrage. San Diego: Code, 2007.

United State of America. Department of the Treasury. Homeowner Affordability and Stability Plan Fact Sheet. 20 Feb. 2009 <http://www.ustreas.gov/news/index2.html>.

The World Almanac and Book of Facts. New York: World Almanac Books, 2007.